Managing in the Next Millennium

Managing in the Next Millennium

Mike Johnson

Butterworth-Heinemann Ltd
Linacre House, Jordan Hill, Oxford OX2 8DP

 A member of the Reed Elsevier plc group

OXFORD   LONDON   BOSTON
MUNICH   NEW DELHI   SINGAPORE   SYDNEY
TOKYO   TORONTO   WELLINGTON

First published 1995

© Management Centre Europe 1995

All rights reserved. No part of this publication may be
reproduced in any material form (including photocopying
or storing in any medium by electronic means and whether
or not transiently or incidentally to some other use of
this publication) without the written permission of the
copyright holder except in accordance with the provisions
of the Copyright, Designs and Patents Act 1988 or under
the terms of a licence issued by the Copyright Licensing
Agency Ltd, 90 Tottenham Court Rd, London, England W1P 9HE.
Applications for the copyright holder's written permission
to reproduce any part of this publication should be
addressed to the publishers.

British Library Cataloguing in Publication Data
Managing in the Next Millennium
    I. Johnson, Mike
    658.400905

ISBN 0 7506 1954 6

Library of Congress Cataloguing in Publication Data
A catalogue record for this book is available from the
Library of Congress

Excerpts on pages 54 and 112 are reprinted by permission
of Harvard Business School Press from Competing for the
Future by Gary Hamel and Pralahad.

Composition by Scribe Design, Gillingham, Kent
Printed and bound in Great Britain by Clays, St. Ives plc

Contents

Preface ix

Acknowledgements xiii

Personal thanks xv

1 **Welcome to the new business world** 1
 More with less 8
 Building for a new century 11
 What to watch for 13
 Insight The twenty-five-year-old warning
 Insight It isn't easy to think ahead
 Insight Ten tipped for tomorrow
 Insight Perceptions of the past

2 **The global world of 2010** 14
 Asia: the great business bonanza 16
 Russia and the CEE 18
 Medium-sized is marvellous 20
 Cultural appreciation 23
 Taking away the fun 27
 The growth industries of the twenty-first century 27
 What to watch for 32
 Insight No name tags!
 Insight More than a grain of truth
 Insight Social forces that impact business tomorrow
 Insight When madness strikes
 Insight Don't forget the developing world

3 **Creating the organization of the next millenium** 34
 A fundamental transformation 35
 Empowerment: not a fad 38
 The market-driven enterprise 40

What's the purpose of your business? 44
The new general manager 46
Law firm, orchestra, or what? 46
Be careful with the culture 51
Embrace constructive tension 56
Change is not an option 56
Starting to like change 58
Confronting the problems 59
What to watch for 61
Insight Innovate, innovate, innovate
Insight Wanted: more internationalism
Insight Goodbye human resources?
Insight Outsource, but don't give away your secrets
Insight Making technology count
Insight The role of the woman manager
Insight Don't waste talent
Insight Not too small

4 **The managers of the next millennium 63**
The new-style manager 67
Autocrat or democrat? 69
The glue of shared values 70
Learning to be executives 71
Multi-tasking abilities 74
Self-managed, self-career directed 75
Exploring the darker side 76
The rewards 77
The manager in society 79
What to watch for 80
Insight Bye, bye Euromanager
Insight English only

5 **The currency of knowledge 82**
Make yourself marketable 83
Education in disarray 84
The bricks and mortar factory 86
MBA blues? 89
The active learning experience 92
No option but to educate 95
What to watch for 96
Insight Learning isn't always formal
Insight Technology will change teaching

6   Cuddling up to the customer   98
The corporate marketing mind-set   99
Moving to market driving   101
No middle-class market   105
Learn to love demanding customers   108
Accountable entrepreneurism   112
What to watch for   115
Insight   Ever closer to the customer
Insight   Here's what you'll have to do
Insight   A word about complacency
Insight   Have an obsession with speed
Insight   What about alliances?

7   Managing the technology of a new millennium   117
Communication is no longer an option   118
The obsolescence of knowledge   121
Don't delegate technology decisions   122
The mobile office   124
The rise of the office cluster   128
Technology for everyone   129
What to watch for   132
Insight   Search for the real competition
Insight   Countries too must compete
Insight   E-mail it
Insight   What office technology can we expect?
Insight   The fourth generation office

8   The new covenant for 2010   133
Earning employee trust   134
Continued development and growth   135
The reward package   137
Survival of the specialists   138
The training burden   142
Manage change – don't let it manage you
What to watch for
Insight   Questions for beginners to the business game
Insight   Be independent!
Insight   Where your pay-packet is going

Conclusion   144

Biographies   146

Preface

The idea for this book developed out of a meeting in London in early 1994 between Kathryn Grant and Jacquie Shanahan of Butterworth-Heinemann, Dom Fanelli and Martin Clarke of Management Centre Europe and myself. The plot was simple: why not use Management Centre Europe's pre-eminence as Europe's leading executive training and development organization to assemble a book that featured inputs from some of its top speakers, seminar and conference leaders? More specifically, why don't we get this broad sweep of talent to collectively look at what every executive good or bad, young or old, is facing – the future?

Managing in the Next Millennium is a powerful package of ideas by some of the world's most renowned and most followed management thinkers and commentators, backed up by input and ideas from management specialists and additional related research.

Predicting business life in the year 2010, the format has been carefully planned to cover the major issues that face executives today in getting ready to survive the business battles of tomorrow.

To make it more interesting than just a simple series of one-on-one interviews or reports, I have taken the thoughts and ideas of these top management thinkers and practitioners and woven them together to build up a picture of how they predict we will manage in the next century.

To make *Managing in the Next Millennium* as useful as possible, and easy to use, there are summaries at the end of each chapter as well as 'signposts' that give clues and direction signs to our collective organizational future.

This book is specifically geared to three groups:

- Top managers will find not only many of their own thoughts and ideas confirmed by some of the leading

management thinkers of our age, but practical ideas on motivation and reward that will be warmly welcomed by their hard-pressed staff.
- Specialists: the new management cadre who are already shaping the organization of the future. This book aims to illustrate how you will work, how you can get the most out of your new empowered role, how you relate to top management.
- New arrivals and business school students: insights into where business is going and how you can best place yourself to take advantage of the new organizational realities that will define the workplace of tomorrow.

Managing in the Next Millennium is designed to help anyone in business stay in business, by sharing the insights and experiences of the very best management brains around. I hope you enjoy reading their thoughts and ideas of how we will work tomorrow.

Mike Johnson
Cartagena, Spain

Acknowledgements

Much of the material that I assembled for *Managing in the Next Millennium* has been based on exclusive one-on-one interviews with some of the most respected names in management. Where it was not always practical to meet face to face, phone and fax interviews were substituted. Additionally, to broaden the base of the book and provide greater coverage of the issues, I have included extracts from keynote presentations at Management Centre Europe's three most important conferences; the International Human Resources Conference, the Global Conference on Marketing and the Top Management Forum. Also, to pick up on specific issues I interviewed a series of additional specialists and have taken extracts from several recent studies and publications.

I would like to personally thank all those who agreed to be interviewed for the book for their enthusiastic involvement and assistance, which is deeply appreciated.

Tom Bonoma, Managing Partner of the Bonoma Group and a former professor at Harvard; Jim Champy, Chairman of CSC Index, co-author of *Re-Engineering the Corporation*; George Day, Professor of Marketing at the Wharton School, University of Pennsylvania; Peter Drucker; John Elkins, President Diefenbach Elkins; Liam Fahey, Adjunct Professor of Strategic Management, Babson College and Professor, Strategic Management, Cranfield School of Management; John Humble; Paul Kahn, Chief Executive, SafeCard Services and former President and CEO, AT&T Universal Card; Mike Kami; T.W. Kang, Managing Director, Global Synergy Associates; Philip Kotler, Professor of International Marketing, Kellogg Graduate School of Management, Northwestern University; Jean-Claude Larréché, Professor of Marketing, INSEAD; Henry Mintzberg; Richard Pascale, business consultant, former member of faculty at the Graduate School of Business, University of Stanford; Michael Porter, Professor of Business Administration,

Harvard Business School; Louis Stern, Professor of Marketing, Kellogg Graduate School of Management, Northwestern University; Lester Thurow, former Dean, Sloan School of Management, Massachusetts Institute of Technology; Paul Tiffany, Professor of Management, the Wharton School, University of Pennsylvania.

Equally I would like to thank other friends of MCE; N. Venkatraman, Associate Professor of Management at Boston University; Sumantra Ghoshal, Professor of Strategy at INSEAD, from whose future-oriented presentations at Management Centre Europe conferences I have reported on extensively and to Gary Hamel of the London Business School and C.K. Prahalad, co-authors of *Competing for the Future* which I quote and Donald Hambrick, Professor of Management at the Graduate School of Management, Columbia University, for comments made in an interview with MCE on Korn-Ferry's study on the manager of the future.

For their input to the book taken from interviews, MCE conference reportage and additional material: Tom Acuff, Managing Partner of Neumann International; Philippe Alloing, Human Resources Director Europe, A.D. Little; Françoise Bacq, consultant, Hewitt CBC; Pier Carlo Falotti, President and Chief Executive, AT&T Europe, Africa, Middle East; Labeed Hamid, President, Middle East Management Centre; Richard Hill, President, Europublic; Theo Lieven, Chairman, Vobis; Wim Noortman, partner, Hansar International; Win Nystrom, Senior Vice-President, PCM Europe Outplacement; Tony Parisi, Director, Human Resources, Central Europe and Middle East, Cigna Insurance; Fearghal Quinn, Chairman, Superquinn; John Seely Brown, Chief Scientist, Xerox Corporation; Mark Thomas, President, Performance Dynamics; David Wimpress, Chairman, Peritas; Nick Winkfield, Director MORI; Michael Winston, Vice-President, Organization and Development, Motorola.

In *Managing the Next Millennium* there are quotes from the following publications:
Competing for the Future by Gary Hamel and C.K. Prahalad, published by Harvard Business School Press
Crowning the Customer – how to become customer-driven by Feargal Quinn, The O'Brien Press, Dublin

Personal thanks

My personal thanks and appreciation for everyone who gave a great deal of their time to this project: Kathryn Grant and Jacquie Shanahan at Butterworth-Heinemann, who were instrumental in getting the project off the ground; Domenico Fanelli, President of AMA International and Martin Clarke, Director of Marketing at Management Centre Europe for giving it their warm support; Karen O'Donnell and Ruth Leahy of MCE's Top Management Programmes Division for getting so many of the interviews arranged – the key to the whole project. Thanks to two old friends; John Humble for reading the draft and for his encouragement and guidance over many years and Peter Spooner for interviews in London and countless glasses of good port. Special thanks to Tom Acuff, Win Nystrom and Mike Staunton for all their input, encouragement and reading of the draft; to Leigh Ann Allard and Fabienne Minguet at J&A for keeping the store open; to Julie Falmagne for putting up with me before, during and after and, finally, to my mother, Joan, who provided the world's best 'hotel' service for three weeks.

1
Welcome to the new business world

> Bad times have a scientific value...we learn geology the morning after the earthquake.
> *Ralph Waldo Emerson*

> An optimist is someone who thinks that the future is uncertain.
> *Anonymous*

In fifteen years time it will be 2010 – a decade into a new millennium, the twenty-first century.

As anyone who has anything to do with business knows there are profound changes taking place right now that will have a lasting impact on what our organizations and our own professional roles will look like. We have all read about the future developments of new materials, of the benefits that biochemistry will bring us, of expected medical breakthroughs, of the world of virtual reality that will let us conceive and plan as never before, of the information super highway – every couch-potato's ultimate dream: access to the whole world without getting out of bed.

But, perhaps more importantly, there are a great number of other, as yet, unknown changes, unforseen developments and discoveries that can easily make a mockery of any attempt to predict even fifteen years hence. All we have to do is turn on our mental camcorder and think of what our professional and private lives were like in 1980 (just fifteen years ago), to see that most experts didn't really have much of a clue; as illustrated in their failure to predict the information explosion of satellites, telecomms and the empowerment of the individual worker that the personal computer has given.

So, if we got it so wrong in 1980, what's going to be different about predicting 2010 and, specifically, the management profession? The answer is nothing at all. There is no way – even at the present pace of technological innovation – that we can really conceive what technology will allow us to do.

But, because the foundations for the next fifteen years are already laid, we can begin to show – and to know – how professional managers as individuals – and the organizations they work for – can arrive in the new world of 2010 still intact. A little bruised maybe, but essentially still fighting fit.

It should be made clear now that the one area that this book does not set out to tackle is any of the geopolitical issues that are the feature of our daily news diet. Predictions of famine, war and pestilence are not part of the scenario, neither are financial markets – they are far too volatile for that. We are in fact assuming a status quo that the world will – one way or another, or one place or another – still be destabilized, to about the same degree.

So anyone expecting an erudite argument on whether Russia will get its economic act together, China will break up into separate trading blocks, South Africa and South America's experiments with democracy will work; or if in our Western world, urban decay, street crime, the drug culture and the break-up of the family will continue, will have to look elsewhere. The only references to these sort of items – important as they are – is when they are seen to have a direct effect on the way we will manage tomorrow.

From the distance of 1995, the road to 2010 may look like a donkey track with a lot of poorly marked paths rather than a superhighway with neon lit directions, but, thanks to some of the world's top management thinkers and commentators, whose insights, ideas and predictions make up this book, we do know a lot about where we are going, how to get there and what it will be like when we do. All we have to do is learn to accept this new working world and learn to profit from it. Unfortunately, as we all know from experience, that is easy to say – difficult to do.

Equally, we have enough information to show how top managers, specialists (we have dropped the phrase 'middle management', as they won't exist in the form they are today in most organizations by 2010) and those just beginning their business career can organize and help themselves to be competitive in the next century and enjoy the challenges that are out there for all of us.

As mentioned earlier, there are some foundations – basic building blocks – already in place, and visible to anyone who cares to take the time to look. They are the supporting columns for the future. Just as a corporate historian could go back to the 1960s, 1970s and 1980s and see the outline of the future, so today's manager can gain a very good idea of where he or she should be going, by reacting to the major trends that are already violently rocking business half-way through the 1990s.

There are five major developments that are already shaping the organization of the future *and* those that work *with* it.

- Companies – large and small – will be global in their operations. That much maligned phrase 'think global, act local' (dubbed 'glocalization') is, in reality, a truism. That means that if you want to play in the big league you had better be the best in the world, not the best in your market. So find out what the best do and learn how to do it better.
- Spurred on by breakthroughs in information technology, the functional, hierarchical organization, that has been the model for most of us for the vast majority of our working lives, will be (and already is being) superseded by the process-based, flat organization. The corporation of eight to twelve levels, will implode to three to five.
- There will be few – if any – jobs for life. Any notion of an implicit contract, if one ever really existed, to provide work for a lifetime between employer and employee is – this very second – being swept away. And as the tide of change recedes it leaves the specialist behind and finally severely curtails the need for the middle manager as we know him or her today. This fundamental change in our working relationships means one very important thing, tomorrow you won't work *for* the firm, you'll work *with* it.

 Start now and focus on the customer...remember, a person isn't a customer until they have bought *twice*!

- There will be a total focus on the customer, practically to the exclusion of all else. Whether your company makes products or provides services, totally satisfying

the customer will be the *obsession* of the successful corporation and the successful manager and the specialists who will support these new – delayered – enterprises. Effective and creative use of information technology (IT) will be the driver of the process.
- As knowledge not currency becomes the 'capital' of tomorrow's enterprise, so continuous learning will be a key to competing. Both corporations and individual executives will have to constantly re-invent themselves.

What all this means is that there are not only major changes and upheavals on the way but *unprecedented opportunities* for managers, executives and entrepreneurs in this new global business society that we have invented for ourselves.

For anyone who reads the business and management press these five 'clues' to tomorrow have been obvious for a long time. The problem is, just as we really knew what we had to do back in the 1980s – when half the professors of Harvard and INSEAD were warning about competition from new quarters and bloated headcounts that would have to be trimmed – are we going to do anything about it?

Right now, as even greater forces come to play on the corporation – bending it out of any shape we recognize – too many of us still haven't done the things that the 1980s demanded never mind considering the next century. And if we haven't already done our homework – or more seriously the organizations we work for haven't done theirs – this lack of action is going to reap bitter rewards in the coming years.

As Paul Tiffany, a professor of management at the Wharton School says gloomily, 'much of modern management can be described as rearranging the deck chairs on the Titanic. One of the great challenges is how do we make managers more aware.'

Not easy. Many managers seem to be operating on the ostrich principle of having their heads in the sand with their most vulnerable parts exposed. This sort of attitude poses very real dangers for thousands of companies all around the globe. Those thousands of companies, employing millions of managers and hundreds of millions of other employees are in trouble. For unless they recognize the changes and do something soon, events will catch up and overwhelm them, making it impossible to compete in this new global world.

> **The twenty-five-year-old warning**
>
> Despite what some say, looking backwards can be useful. It can also be a salutary lesson. Twenty-five years ago futurologist Alvin Toffler wrote the best-selling book *Future Shock* and put the clues to today's chaos right under our noses – if we had bothered to do anything about it.
>   Tofler's view from back in 1970 was pretty accurate to say the least.
>   'In three short decades between now and the twenty-first century, millions of ordinary, psychologically normal people will face an abrupt collision with the future. Citizens of the world's richest and most technologically advanced nations, many of them will find it increasingly painful to keep up with the incessant demand for change that characterizes our time. For them the future will have arrived too soon.'

Indeed, so worrying is this lack of action as we go through this major work revolution that as Paul Tiffany suggests 'no one's managing change, at best they are trying to keep up'.

What frustrates Tiffany and others like him is that much management is still done on what he terms the 'BFO theory – blinding flashes of the obvious'.

Possibly one of the difficulties is that with so much change going on – and we must accept that it is now well understood that change is the status quo, and a new age of stability is not around the corner – many managers are frustrated that what they consider their best efforts frequently come to nothing. Increasing your work time, trying harder than ever only to stand still can be very off-putting for many managers. Additionally, many, used to a more genteel business existence, find it practically impossible to either understand the need for, or make, major change.

But, no one is holding out any hope that the world is going to stop reshaping itself. Everyone has to understand that a fundamental metamorphosis is going on. One of the world's leading commentators on management issues, Michael Porter, of Harvard Business School, says 'The forces reshaping the way companies work are going on and on and we see no relief in sight.'

So anyone expecting to wake up one day and find that the sun's out and it's all plain sailing and calm waters again had better not hold out too much hope.

All the same, for anyone who welcomes a white water ride the new tomorrow is going to be an exciting place: something akin to the executive version of bungee jumping – taking a leap into the unknown and hoping all will be well. But don't totally despair. As history has shown us, we are all extremely adaptable to new surroundings, new climates, new requirements. That at least, is the good bit. The bad part is that if we don't adapt the next generation (some of them are reading this book) *will*. Computer literate, totally at home in a world where change is the constant, they are the ones to worry about, not change itself.

Even if some of us will eventually get to like it and embrace it as the new status quo, all this change, change, change prompts a wry comment on the futility of long-range plans in an age of change from the doyen of management thinkers. Peter Drucker – whose ideas of the future organizational make-up of our corporations take up much of this book – says 'if plans fail you have succeeded, if plans succeed you have failed'.

What Drucker is offering is not just a lot more confusion and a lot more chaos, but an opportunity to learn that the idea of change as a constant feature of working life, can make the new working world an exciting, enervating place to be.

 Think about your business five years ago ... if you are still working the same way you are probably in trouble.

Indeed, many managers have already got used to the mayhem that seems to make up life from Monday to Friday these days and have learned to love it, be excited and transformed by it.

All told, it isn't really something for us to get despondent about (as the business magazines and the newspapers would perhaps seem to suggest) it is something for us to learn about, live with, and plan for. If plans don't work, plan for them not too, make yourself and your organization change-proof by making change part of your daily business life.

> **It isn't easy to think ahead**
>
> In 1985, Swiss-based executive search firm TASA published a research document titled, *The Manager of the Year 2000*, based on interviews with a broad cross-section of senior managers. Updated by ten years – to 2010 – the introduction to the research could be a text of today.
>
> 'It is not easy to get hard-working practical managers to think ahead almost fifteen years – long-range planning is out of fashion – and practically impossible, these days, to find anyone daring to predict the future; too many intelligent managers are still shell-shocked from a decade of economic roller-coaster rides. Perhaps it was personal experience of seeing their own corporate planners suffering top management wrath when they got it wrong – again. As one said, 'If anyone in the 1960s had told you what the 1980s would really be like, you'd have said they were crazy.' What would they say today about some of the wild predictions we really should be making about the next fifteen years?

And this really does mean embracing the fact that change is not just something that pops up every now and then, and then goes away for a decade or so – but a linear process that never stops. We can stop, we can stay in one place, but the business we are in won't.

Tony Parisi, a human resource manager at insurance giant Cigna in Brussels gives a 'troops in the trenches' view. 'If I close my eyes and think about what I was doing – what my company was doing – just four years ago I'm really now in a different job, doing different things in a different company.'

And compounding this problem of adapting to constant change, is that top managers – even the very best who see the need for change and are already doing something about it – are often struggling to sail in the right direction. Beset by storms, buffeted by the enemy, they seem to spend more and more time just keeping the corporate ship afloat.

This has resulted, as times have got progressively harder, in management taking it out on the workforce. There can be few senior managers anywhere these days who haven't demanded more and more productivity from a dwindling, down-sized workforce. Whether they should feel guilty or not is another matter. Most managers justify the tightening of the productivity screw as inevitable. The alternative, they say, is to go out of business. But what is certain, is that there are not many executives enjoying business life to the full these days.

As Liam Fahey, a strategic management professor at Babson College in the USA and Cranfield School of Management in the UK points out, 'it's hard to find people who are enjoying themselves in management. The challenge for corporations is how do you inspire people to do the best for the corporation. A lot of people leave because they feel they could do it better themselves.'

More with less

Today when managers leave of their own volition or as a victim of downsizing, the ones who are left behind are being asked to crank up the productivity levels to new highs. 'More with less' is the battle cry of many hard-pressed corporations. And when the boat is being blown in several directions at once, it's difficult to keep your feet, never mind your sense of direction. Wherever you look, in North America, across Europe, even in Japan, fewer and fewer managers are being asked to take on more and more. In some companies – seriously wounded by recession and changing market conditions – one manager is doing the work of four or five. That stress, coupled to the uncertainty of what will happen next is putting a major strain on many corporations.

Learning to manage that – in tough times – and still get the very best from the workforce is a new, exciting business challenge for many: but it is one that must be met.

However, the necessary get-tough policies of many companies could well backfire and some observers firmly believe that all the pressure heaped onto those left on board is going to lead to a tough day of reckoning in the near future. UK-based organizational consultant, Mark Thomas says 'I detect a huge mountain of pent-up labour turnover amongst Europe's managers. Against the vicious recessionary background and the constant threat of job losses many managers are massively disenchanted with the "more and more with less and less" philosophy of employers. Many managers believe that any change has to be better than what they have currently got. In my experience the question, "have you got your CV ready?" brings wry smiles. Loyalty is for most managers a redundant term, indeed many are beginning to recognize that the only loyalty they should have is to themselves.'

Danger signal: key executives are on the move again. Now's the time to go the extra distance to make sure your team stays intact.

Thomas continues, 'I believe that many managers will be enacting swift revenge and exiting from employers whose attitude has been less than motivational. Employers have to start working hard at motivating staff and providing a sense of purpose to people. New forms of real reward and development will provide some of the answers.'

Thomas's point is perhaps prophetic. Just a few months after he made the comment, there are already strong signs of people on the move. During the last five years employees have stayed huddled in their positions – hunkered down in the trenches – hoping that the next round of downsizing will miss them if they keep out of sight. Now, they are beginning to emerge into the open. For as most career-minded managers know, if they stay in a lacklustre position for too long they will be stuck there. Not forever, just long enough for their lack of use to the corporation to be discovered.

So now is the time to make a break for it and get into a new job, in a new organization before it's too late, or show your current boss what you can really do: even take risks occasionally. And look at it this way, if this does turn into a widespread revolt, life on the corporate front line is going to be very interesting indeed over the next couple of years.

As an example, if serving the customer is held up as the great truth of tomorrow's success, how do you do that with less than really motivated people. How can anyone expect to keep the customer coming back if they are being served or advised by employees who have lost the will to care?

As the leading management commentator Henry Mintzberg observes 'there are two major and contradictory tendencies.

> **Ten tipped for tomorrow**
>
> In 1994 a poll by the Economist Intelligence Unit of 600 senior executives found that leadership was the key attribute to managing global business in the year 2000. Furthermore, it asked the 600 to list the people who they felt were best suited to lead a corporation into the next century, based on a commitment to the customer, an ability to inspire and coach every worker to top performance, constant encouragement of new ideas and a disdain for the status quo.
>
> The top ten were: Jack Welch, General Electric; George Fisher, Eastman Kodak; Percy Barnevik, ABB; Bill Gates, Microsoft; Richard Branson, Virgin Atlantic; Lee Iacocca, Chrysler; Dennis Weatherstone, JP Morgan; Roy Vagelos, Merck; John Sculley, formerly with Apple; Robert Allen, AT&T.
>
> Just how long many of these top ten business gladiators will really be leading above and beyond the year 2000 is doubtful. In 2010 two of them will be in their eighties, and four in their seventies. Even the 'ageless schoolboy' Richard Branson will be 59 and Microsoft's Gates a greying 54.
>
> If these leaders of today and others like them – regardless of their qualities – are regarded as the people we will be looking up to in the next century, we had better start looking for some new blood soon, or business is going to be in more trouble than most of us think.

The first is involve people and make them belong, the second is kick them out and make the organization more mercenary. It's having a devastating effect on dealing with customers – but we talk about offering service!'

So, no one is saying that getting people motivated, getting them to love the customer while the corporation is in upheaval is going to be easy, but it has to be done. How to get demotivated staff to do things even if they know that the alternative is possibly joining the ranks of redundant middle managers is going to be a key skill – a challenging but potentially rewarding task – in the future; but one that many managers still have to learn.

Noting just how far we have come in the last decade, and the changes that have already happened, Lester Thurow,

> **Perceptions of the past**
>
> That master of management thinking, Peter Drucker, referred to our perceptions of the past and future as firmly fixed in our own experiences. 'My granddaughter can comprehend that we didn't have television,' he said during a recent lecture, 'but she couldn't understand that we didn't have elastic bands!'
>   A future generation in 2010 will perhaps appreciate that we didn't have instant voice-activated real time video communication, but be surprised that 3M's Post-it notes were an invention of the late 1980s.

former Dean of the Sloan School of Management at MIT, jokes 'Suppose in 1989 God had told the truth about what would happen in 1994, he wouldn't have been able to do anything about it because the staff wouldn't have done it.'

Thurow's right. The profound changes that have been wrought over the last five years or so have left many – even in senior positions – doubting reality and gasping for breath.

Therefore, it is important for all of us to take a good cold, pragmatic shower, when it comes to considering our response to the need for better and better customer service. Let's all abandon the rosy vision from the textbooks of happy, smiling, 'Have a nice day, sir' employees – that's not who we are dealing with, not who we are managing. We are not going to be dealing with a group of highly motivated people. We are going to be dealing with the same group of people as always, some more enthusiastic than others. How we make them do a better job, how we get them to accept that things can get better, is what managers have to make their main role in life: creating a new organizational culture that fits this post-downsized society.

Building for a new century

So today, amid the ruin and the wreckage, it is a time to be more optimistic, and be certain that there has to be a way – after all the cut, cut, cut culture – to build new organizations for a new century.

As Paul Kahn, former President and CEO of AT&T Universal Card and now CEO at SafeCard Services says, 'people are hungry for people to care about them. There are no other icons any more, government, the law, the church, the family are no longer the support they were. I look at what we have now as an opportunity to create an icon in business, that will make people enjoy coming to work again, make them perform better and give them something back.'

Certainly, many employees think they deserve something from their corporations for all the hard work they have done in an exceedingly rocky environment. Just being glad to have a job – especially as we come out of recession – isn't going to be quite enough.

And with a corporate roller-coaster ride in permanent progress, many hard-pressed managers may be forgiven for doubting that the future that Kahn and others paint can be a reality. Yet if corporations – or individual executives – are going to get to 2010, they are going to have to deal with these issues and get them right. So as we stagger up the long climb to 2010, there are messages for all of us that we must understand if we are to survive:

- *For top managers* You must build new bridges with the people you work with, and that includes suppliers. Motivation to work and a sense of purpose must be put back into organizations as a matter of urgency.
- *For specialists* If you still think you're a middle manager, you're a dead duck! Whatever you do must be special, you must differentiate yourself from your colleagues and make 'employability' your watchword.
- *For those just getting onto the executive ladder* Assuming you don't want to jump off right now and pick what is sure to be a different, more peaceful profession, learn to read the signs on the rocky road to the future. Don't let yourself get institutionalized and tied down by promises. Keep learning every day and don't ever get too comfy.

That is the broad picture. Not necessarily beautiful, but all we have to work with: and a lot clearer in reality than it was even five years ago.

Remember, it needn't be a disaster scenario. In many ways all the doom and gloom (the 'it's going to get worse before it gets better' syndrome) is over ... the ghosts have been exorcised. Now is the time to build, to develop yourself and the business you work with, to meet and welcome those new challenges – the challenges of a new business world.

That's why in the next chapter we find out how all the experts predict we are going to get to the world of tomorrow and what we will have to do when we get there.

What to watch for

- 'Think global and act local' may sound like a silly slogan but not only is it true, smart corporations are already making it work for them. Shouldn't you make it work for you too?
- As the 'concrete middle' of executive hierarchies collapses, organizations are already leaner, meaner and above all *flatter*. News gets to the top *fast* ... people know what customers *really* want. Examine your organization. Does it hoard information or share it?
- There are no jobs for life. You can't expect it and the company won't offer it, no matter how senior you are. The best jobs will go to the best qualified, and those who keep up-to-date. What are your plans for staying employable? Sit down and make them now.
- Everyone says the customer is the focus for the future. How customer focused are you? How customer focused is your company? If you answer 'not very' to either, you're in trouble already.
- Knowledge – lots of it now, and lots more later – is the key to future success. Start making plans to be a knowledge worker – from today.
- All the same the challenge is, and will be, very exciting indeed for those ready to play the game. New rules, new ideas, new markets: everything is in place for those of us with potential – and those businesses with potential – to succeed.

2

The global world of 2010

> If you have too many problems maybe you should go out of business. There is no law that says a company must last forever
>
> *Peter Drucker*
>
> If you don't do it excellently, don't do it at all. Because, if it's not excellent it won't be profitable or fun. And if you're not in business for fun or profit, what the hell are you doing there?
>
> *Robert Townsend* (author of *Up the Organization*)

The Global Village exists. Whether we like it or not – whether we want to work that way or not – we are in an age of practically instant communications from anywhere to anywhere. As E-mail, worldphone cards, computerized call-backs and video-conferencing have shown, the only thing you need to be an instant global player is a few thousand dollars. For a few thousand more you can buy a dish that will up-link you to a satellite and you can work from the centre of Borneo if that is what takes your fancy. For any serious business executive, already today, the phrase 'Sorry I wasn't in when you phoned' is the most lame excuse in the vocabulary. By tomorrow it will be as hackneyed as 'Your cheque's in the mail,' or 'Our computers have just gone down.'

Therefore, the successful corporations of the next century will be those who make the decision today to join in the global business battle and get 'in touch' with what the best practice companies are doing right now. What they are doing is scouting the world for anything and everything that can give them an edge on the competition. People, products, ideas are all becoming world commodities, key parts of the corporate armoury for tomorrow's battles for market turf.

For, whatever else there will be in the brave new century, globalization is going to take the lead in shaping the way our companies do business, the way we do business and the way each and every one of us works. Don't think that you cannot be affected. No matter how small your business, someone, somewhere across the globe has a process, a product, a plan that will affect you personally. It might be a new piece of technology that can revolutionize how you produce, it might be a new product that you can add to your exiting lines, it might be a new, cheaper way of doing what you think you do quite efficiently. Whatever it is, you can bet, if you are in business, something like that is going to happen. Whether you take advantage of it or not is up to you.

Consultant and author John Humble comments, 'Business just has to become ever more global. Most things can be made anywhere by anybody as the knowledge increasingly flows globally to make this possible.'

But Humble warns of rushing blindly out to the market with the worldwide widget. 'Thinking global and making global doesn't mean marketing global. Think globally but market locally, that will be the right approach.'

Peter Drucker feels that the globalization of the business part of our world at least is practically complete in that 'we have become a world without any one permanent centre'. Others feel that we are in a tri-polar world (North America, Europe and Asia), where differences – particularly cultural – still strongly prevail, and will do so for some time to come.

Interestingly, the Asian viewpoint is slightly different. Many business experts there see not a single world or a tri-polar world, but a bi-polar. Tokyo-based T.W. Kang, author of the highly acclaimed book *Gaishi – the Foreign Company in Japan* comments, 'There is no doubt that an increasingly uncertain geopolitical environment will continue to persist. If one thinks about two of the most significant events in Asia that will take place before the advent of the twenty-first century – the return of Hong Kong to China and the 'reunification of the Korean peninsula – one can see that the managerial environment becomes bipolar.'

From Kang's perspective this raises an interesting challenge for the global business at either pole. 'You can either take advantage of the opportunities that such discontinuities bring by looking for imperfections' he says, 'or one can be passive and suffer the consequences. That is why we must learn how to find the imperfections and to be able to react in a relatively spontaneous fashion.'

That is part of what all of us should be working on right now. Looking for new ways, new ideas and new thinking that can get our organization and lift it out of the pack, setting it on a secure road for tomorrow. And as those competing blocks begin to either fall apart or simply melt into one, opportunities will abound.

The disappearance of geographical trading blocks is also forecasted by John Elkins, a founder of the corporate strategy firm Diefenbach Elkins, who supports Drucker's theory, saying that 'the concept of competing economic blocks will fall apart. They will all blur over a period of time.'

Neither does Elkins rate the chances of the Japanese all that much in the next fifteen years. 'I think they will be limited in what they can do,' he says, 'they are still very isolationist, very reluctant to take their place in the world.'

Asia: the great business bonanza

With Asia clearly confirmed as what strategic management professor Liam Fahey terms, 'the last great bonanza' and one that will 'change the face and ideas of corporations', the battle lines being drawn now, for a showdown as the new century dawns will be decisive.

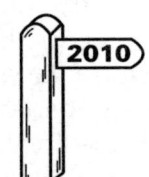

Warning signal: Don't be fooled about Asia as the region that will solve the West's worries. It'll be a tough battle, but well worth the effort for those who are prepared to work at it.

All the same, don't think that Asia is going to be an easy market to play in. Fahey suggests that wily governments in Asia have learned either from their own bitter experiences, or watching the experiences of others, that you don't just let a multinational come and play in your backyard with no strings attached. 'Companies will have to go to these markets and create local involvement,' says Fahey, indicating that simple 'screwdriver', local assembly operations won't work. To build faith with the government and the local community there will have to be more than that. 'Experience and culture won't let

> **No name tags!**
>
> If medium-sized is the model for the future corporation, Peter Drucker reckons there is a simple test to tell if you've got too big. 'You know your business isn't medium-sized when you have to wear a name-tag to the company sales conference!'

Asia or Brazil do what countries like Ireland and Scotland did in the 1950s and 1960s,' Fahey declares, referring to inward investment at almost any price. 'Nations will want to have power over their own decisions,' he forecasts, 'not have companies making their own decisions and holding power over local communities. Places like India and China have been really careful to date,' he notes, 'and will continue to be careful.'

This raises the important issue that to do business in the future, managers from the West will have to understand local needs and culture to a much greater degree than they do now. Bringing to their job a real appreciation of the differences in these markets.

Still, pleasing those you need to do business with will have a lot of upsides. Although China is most often quoted as the next big market – frequently on population terms alone, which fail to link that to any idea of spendable income – India is probably the bumper bonanza of the next fifteen years if import barriers tumble. Enthuses Fahey, 'India has probably more middle class than the whole of the total population of the USA and Canada put together. When you consider that these millions [some put it as high as 150 million] have been starved of consumer products – but have the money to buy – you can imagine the battles to come, as corporations like Volkswagen, Ford, Toyota, McDonalds, Pizza Hut and Burger King fight each other for this precious piece of market turf.

As none of us can know exactly what the world's stage is going to look like in 2010, strategist John Elkins suggests that the way to manage it is to have a vision for your global ambitions. 'Companies are not going to look out more than ten years. That's ten years for the vision and only two years for measuring how you are really doing and how the environment around you is changing. I would urge people to put a stake in the ground ten years out – but be flexible.'

Elkins points out that, 'five-year planning cycles are really a waste of time. They are not far enough out to be subjective and communicate a vision, not close enough to be measurable.'

Using a golfing analogy, Elkins argues that it's 'just like putting. Far out you may get lucky, close up it's easy. Five years is just tricky and you often miss.'

When you talk to beleaguered managers these days, some feel that even five months out is tough to get right. Trying to entice or encourage them to fly a flag ten years out is not what they really want to hear right now. All the same, someone, somewhere has to start the process. Getting smart about the future is becoming a major imperative.

Say that to a manager who has just learned to focus on short-term action for mid-term survival and you are likely to be met with incredulous looks. All the same, Elkins is right on the mark. If you don't have an idea, you don't have a vision or some sort of long-term plan, how will you know when it goes wrong?

Russia and the CEE

With Asia – including India – and South America being touted as the last bastions of freewheeling market opportunity, what about Russia and Central and Eastern Europe as targets for global corporate ambition? Despite some heady reporting of successes and profits, enthusiasm for these areas is mixed at best. Most experts regard the three best performing countries, the Czech Republic, Poland and Hungary as doing very well (but getting a little carried away with their own success), however their relative size puts them down the list as mega-market opportunities. Russia and the independent republics are seen as a high risk affair – particularly until a rule of law – that includes an enforceable contract law and protection of intellectual property – is properly established and imposed.

The bigger concern for the next century that the former communist bloc creates is that, if private enterprise does not join with governments in the West to improve working opportunities in the region, there will be a continual loss of jobs. This will create an emigration to the more affluent West (see box). Peter Drucker warns, 'We must put jobs in Eastern Europe, put

> **More than a grain of truth**
>
> As an example of how changing world conditions can seriously affect the future of markets, MIT Sloan School's former Dean, Lester Thurow, uses the example of the Ukraine and its agricultural potential. This illustration, and its implications for the next century strikes terror into management conference delegates around the globe.
>
> 'A little bit of history. Who was the world's largest producer and exporter of grain in the 19th century? It was the Ukraine and the area around it, which is the best place for growing grain on the face of the earth. Good soil, good rainfall and a perfect transportation system of rivers to the Black Sea, so everything goes out on cheap water transportation. The Ukraine does not have its act together, but when it does and says who owns the land, then if I am John Deere or Fiat – the two largest makers of farm machinery in the world – I am going to organize some kind of credit arrangement. Lend them the money to buy farm machinery, barter grain back in return and sell it on the world grain market. And I am going to drive grain farmers in Europe, America and Australia out of business. In any market economy you won't grow grain in Montana, it will be grown in the Ukraine. In Europe, you have a simple choice. French and Spanish grain farmers can go out of business or you will find a million Ukrainians living in Paris.'
>
> As executives operating on a world stage, he suggests we must be aware of these issues, learn from them and be able to take advantage of them, by positioning in the right place at the right time, otherwise we will surrender yet another advantage to our global competition.

work there, build factories there or eastern emperors will be in Western Europe. There is no way of keeping them out, there are masses of people who are trainable, but have not been trained.'

Drucker hammers home the need for all of us to think global like this, 'Businesses in a great majority of places will *not* serve local markets, regional markets or very narrow markets. Every executive already, let alone in the next millennium, needs to learn to think globally, to try and keep himself or herself informed globally; to respond in his business and in his own activity to the global challenges.'

Drucker adds a point that we all know, but often choose to forget, 'The successful executive of the next millennium will have to realize that money and information are not national and are totally out of the control of any political system we have, but – above all – he will have to realize that what happens in the most remote corner of the world may tomorrow have an impact on his own local market, he should realize that already there is no economic centre.'

Medium-sized is marvellous

From that, Drucker goes on to conclude that, to meet the tough conditions of tomorrow our organizations will have to be not just leaner, meaner, but driven by intelligence and knowledge. Challenging the idea that the big business model is still what we should look up to as the symbol of future success, he suggests a new shape that will dominate the corporation of tomorrow: medium-sized enterprises. 'The overwhelming majority of businesses tomorrow will not be big businesses, they will be small and medium-sized businesses,' he says.

And picking up on earlier advice he warns, 'Even the smallest and most local of them will have to learn to think globally, to inform itself globally, to realize that it operates in an economy that no longer has any boundaries.'

 Medium-sized companies are going to be the winners in the next millennium.

The idea of mid-sized business being right for tomorrow's challenges is supported by Drucker's old friend John Humble, who points out that we should have worked this out for ourselves already as it is clearly this sector of the market that is driving most economies out of recession.

Humble says, 'Thinking about the survival of business into the twenty-first century, too many of us make the mistake of thinking about big business. But, managers running small and medium-sized businesses live their lives in the front line. They don't need to read a book to know that customer satisfaction matters or go to a seminar to be told that cash-flow matters.'

Many leaders of multinationals would agree with Humble. Forced to trim the fat from the corporate carcass, forced to try and understand the markets they have lost touch with, they can be forgiven for looking enviously at the fast moving, innovative smaller corporations that have been snapping at their heels. As lay-offs in many industries continue, with even more forecast for the future, big business is having its hardest time since the recessionary 1930s.

And it is because many of the giants are slowing and showing their old age that Humble believes that, 'small and medium businesses are increasingly the powerhouse of the economy'. His view is shared by Harvard's Michael Porter who suggests that, 'maybe Germany, with its medium-sized companies is a better bet. Remember, the goal of the German company is to exist forever. Compare that to the typical British or US company which is in business to maximize today's stock price.'

Porter continues, 'OK there are some industries in which scale is tremendously important. I mean if you are going to make commercial airplanes there is basically only room for a couple of those companies in the world – maybe three. But that is the example everyone uses. I go to hundreds of companies in hundreds of industries and let me tell you in most industries the scale of economies are going down not up.'

Porter explains, 'Modern, flexible information technology, intense manufacturing processes, combined with a greater use of outside suppliers have driven, substantially the scale of economies down.' This truly is a death knell for the multinational monolith unable, unwilling or incapable of putting its house in order. While others have downsized and trimmed their operations to a sleek, well-honed core, and other medium-sized companies have entered as aggressive new players, they are left to flounder and ultimately founder, victims of their own hugeness.

Picking up on that trend, Porter forecasts a possible funeral somewhere down the fifteen-year path to 2010 for the big company that does not look out. 'In business after business that I work in, we have learnt that we don't have to make everything inside the company – we can let specialist outside suppliers do it. Remember, often the need to be big was a function not of the core product, but of the inputs you were buying or making in-house. But, most importantly, scale is being defeated by the pace of change. Today we find that you can be very efficient in doing what was done in the past – but that doesn't get you very much. The big company of today is not being defeated by another big company, but by small companies.'

And Porter goes on to show that a fundamental change in the process of business is likely to leave the big corporation high and dry and gasping on the beach. 'Small companies,' Porter points out, 'are more dynamic, are more innovative, they can change rapidly. You know IBM lost out to Compaq and Sun Microsystems, both small companies. What IBM was doing was quite efficient, but what they were doing was irrelevant. That's the nature of modern, international competition. As information flows very rapidly, as companies compete globally, inputs and scale are no longer a competitive advantage. If that's what you're hoping then you are in trouble. Today the paradigm of competition has shifted to a paradigm based on progress. Competitive advantage today results not from anything that's static but from the capacity of the organization to continuously improve and, even more importantly to innovate.'

For companies, small *isn't* beautiful. You cannot know enough to be successful.

Thinking about how we are going to get to 2010 in any sort of reasonable condition Peter Drucker concurs on the optimum size of the future corporation, 'realize that in a world that is changing fast – in which information and money have become globally available, there is no more advantage in being big. This is a world for the medium-sized. Don't say small. The truly small business is probably at a disadvantage, simply because it cannot know enough. But the medium-sized business – what the Germans call the 'mittelstant' – that may be the business that is best positioned, because it knows its markets, it knows its customers and yet it is big enough to do whatever is needed technically in terms of training people, of paying people, in terms of investing for five years in an experiment.'

Let's take a moment to explain small. Probably anything under 50 people, where there just cannot, physically be enough people on the ground, not enough hours in the day to really penetrate a market and cause an upset to a better prepared competitor.

Cultural appreciation

Another issue for the global marketer is the rise of what Paul Tiffany calls 'ethnic civilizations', where markets in the global sense are defined more by cultures or religions that cross national boundaries. Referred to by Peter Drucker as the 'pressure toward tribalism' it will greatly affect how we market, what those segments look like and how we create a marketing message.

Liam Fahey thinks this is a very important aspect of the future that the corporation with global aspirations must fully understand: it cannot sit in one place and try to manage anymore. As he points out, 'If you stop and think about it, the 1970s-style US corporation is a dinosaur. The notion of having, say, a Westinghouse in Pittsburgh making decisions for around the world is just about laughable. Equally, the assumption that you can send managers out for a couple of years and they know how to run things doesn't work either.'

Fahey and others see that organizations of tomorrow must be culturally aware in new ways. They must be able to understand the local markets and have people who represent the markets they are in. In Fahey's eyes truly global means ultimately a world management team. 'Imagine,' he suggests, 'a Japanese firm in 2010 with a bunch of non Japanese at the top with their headquarters in Dusseldorf.'

Whether that will remain a dream for the foreseeable future remains to be seen, but there is certainly a need for managements – particularly top managements – to take a long, hard look at the way they approach markets now and in the future. Ethnic, religious and cultural mixes have already created a veritable pot-pourri of new markets and niches, many of which take considerable local understanding to begin to get close to.

Another view of Liam Fahey's vision of a multi-ethnic corporation is proposed by the *enfant terrible* of business commentators, Mike Kami, who has said more irreverent things

Social forces that impact business tomorrow

Although changing social forces are not really a central part of this look into the future of the organization, there are a considerable number of issues that will drastically impact each and every business over the next fifteen years. So it is vital that managers keep these big external issues in mind as we head toward the next millennium. Failure to appreciate, understand, prepare for and react to major societal forces can have a serious or quite possible terminal effect on the bottom line of any business.

> You must stay aware of the big, global issues. One way or another they will affect your business.

- The welfare state – particularly in Europe – is in crisis. Flagging economies, increasingly ageing populations and abuses of the system have left politicians and civil servants at a loss for what to do. So look for increased pressure on companies to up their social contributions and make companies more responsible for medical and retirement cover. While companies may see this as yet another burden on already high wage costs, the brightest will see that offering attractive – and innovative – non-salary benefits as a 'carrot' can attract the best people.
- Environmental issues are becoming paramount and a major part of political platforms of parties of all colours. Business will have to learn self-regulation or face the consequences of new laws that politicians will be urged to introduce by electorates who rightly expect a greener world. Companies should consider doing two things: first, become cleaner and greener on your own (even if you are only a service organization this is still possible), don't wait for the legislation to catch up; second, find ways to turn your environmental attitude into an advantage for you by becoming a market leader of a process, a product or a service. Being environmentally sound doesn't only mean cost, it brings marketing opportunities as well.

continued

- Large scale immigration has changed the cultural, religious and racial mix of many countries. New immigration from countries in the former Soviet Union and Central and Eastern Europe (CEE) is creating a new – work at any price – underclass in Western Europe. In the USA by the turn of the century only 57 percent of the people entering the workforce will be native born whites. An implication for managers is that we must all get used to managing an ethnically-mixed workforce in our own home countries.
- Our political leaders seem unable to solve the chronic unemployment that bedevils most of Europe. High – in excess of 10 percent – unemployment seems set to continue well into the next century – and could be further fuelled by illegal immigrants from both the CEE and North Africa. And it is not only the northern countries that are being impacted either. Countries like Spain already have an underclass of thousands of illegal labourers from North Africa working in the fields: a fact not conducive to easing an unemployment level of more than 20 per cent. As consultant and author John Humble reflects, 'The dream that everyone was entitled to a full-time job – that hard work would bring about a better quality of life than one's parents – has turned out to be, literally, a waking nightmare for many.'
- The Western image of the nuclear family of father, mother, two children and a dog, beloved by the advertising industry is breaking up in many Western states. Single parents make up a quarter of London's population, and life without a permanent partner is increasingly common elsewhere. Equally, the aged are the ones with the money to spend.

What this means, in the mature markets at least, is that the elderly are out to have a ball. After all they know they can't take it with them, so why not do all the things they always wanted to, but never had the time to try.

So, if it might be your last drink, you're going to have Black Label not the Red. If it's your last car, you'll make sure you have all the options you can get.

Marketers and others must monitor these demographic changes which will fundamentally change

continued

> **INSIGHT**
>
> *(from previous page)*
> customer habits and needs, or face the consequences that someone else faster and more innovative (or just plain hungry) will.
> - With the cold war over, the arms industry is no longer the world's number one: it has been overtaken by drugs. Drug abuse – coupled to related crime – is a major social issue that will touch all of us one way or another. A US security industry executive described the twenty-first century as 'a world where one third of the population, protects a second third, from the other third.'

about management failure than anyone. 'Globalization is certainly the route we are taking, there will be no provincialism,' he assures us. 'So chauvinism is out. Or is it? This is where the inner psyche of top managers becomes very important.'

But Kami is certain that, sooner or later top managements will have to make that choice. As he says, 'The corporation with the least prejudices will be the winner.' Look inside the corporation that you currently work for. How few prejudices has it?

While others are not sure that this will happen (see Chapter 3) it holds out a lot of possibilities as we move towards a new century. But, even now, globalization is causing problems of another sort.

Jim Champy, widely regarded as the leading exponent and documenter of the re-engineering trend that is sweeping our corporations, suggests, 'With global competition you'll have to be better at your core business processes than companies in other countries or regions, whether it's concept to market, customer acquisition or customer service.'

To do this, Champy suggests, 'the workforce will have to be more pluralistic. So managers will have to deal with diversity. They will have to understand other cultures and how people from other places think and work – and how to make them work for you. And because of global customers, managers will have to learn how to make the same or similar core business processes work across difficult cultures.'

One area where these trends are perhaps not fully appreciated for some is in marketing. Whether you believe that a company can build a global brand from scratch these days, that works the same way in every market (most observers think not, hence the 'be global, act local' mantra that marketers chant every morning while they shave or put on their make-up), some are still trying. That, coupled with downsizing, has had a crippling effect on local (national or regional) marketing departments.

Jean-Claude Larréché, Professor of Marketing at INSEAD, observes, 'What high performers seem to have more and more difficulty in finding among potential employers is the freedom to act, experiment and learn.'

Taking away the fun

That is bad enough, but the rest is worse, 'For instance, globalization of marketing is taking more and more of the fun away from local marketing teams. Many talented marketing executives leave the subsidiaries of firms going the globalization route to join the subsidiaries of other corporations which still believe in the virtue of decentralized local marketing.'

Maybe here is a dilemma that is only able to be solved by facing the fact four square that – with few exceptions – a global product cannot be marketed the same way in this new world we inhabit. But, if global is the way to go, and if the middle-sized company is the way to do it, won't there be more and more opportunities for the bright, attuned marketing man or woman, who knows how to take a product and service and turn it into a saleable commodity or idea in Saigon, Seattle or Stockholm?

The growth industries of the twenty-first century

And if you want to be a real success you had better not just pick the right countries to be in, you had better read in the global tarot cards or tea-leaves of tomorrow which industries will grow and why.

During a discussion with senior managers in London in 1994, Peter Drucker pointed out that there had been four big industries in the past: leisure, healthcare, education and commercial banking. For the world of tomorrow, the picture – in his view – was somewhat different.

When madness strikes

Economist Lester Thurow spends a lot of time on the global lecture circuit these days. Most of that time is spent warning senior executives and others that it isn't sufficient just to look to the future, a good dose of history can help us see trends, opportunities and pitfalls as well.

One of Thurow's recent messages is to watch carefully what is really going on in your time frame and apply the lessons you learn to your future business planning, it can save you a lot of grief later.

Says Thurow, 'It's a mistake to think of us as recovering from recession. Technically that's correct, but generically that's not what we're doing. We're doing something much more fundamental, because periodically, in the history of capitalism, capitalists go stark raving mad. They do things which people look back historically and say, "How can any sane, sensible human being ever have done it?" We identify these periods as manias and bubbles, and everyone knows the famous names – Tulip Mania, the South Sea Bubble, the Mississippi Land Bubble, the Roaring Twenties.

'At the peak of Tulip Mania in Holland in the 1620s, you could trade one tulip bulb in Amsterdam for fifty-six homes. Think about that. And everybody says, "How could any sane, sensible human being ever have done it?" But they didn't do it once, they did it about every sixty or eighty years. Now if you look at these manias and bubbles, they last for about a decade. They always end up in a financial crash and then you have a lengthy period of cleaning up the mess, which is also usually about a decade. If one looks at the economy at the beginning of the bubble and then twenty years later, after you've cleaned up the mess it's a very different economy.

'Now if one thinks about these colourful names like Tulip Mania and the Roaring Twenties the fact of the matter is that these names were not used at that time. Those names were coined by historians. For example, the Roaring Twenties is a phrase that was first used in 1939, ten years after it was over, because you didn't know it was the Roaring Twenties until it quit roaring! Of course the Roaring Twenties ended with the Kreditanstalt crash in Europe and the stock market crash in the USA and the ten years of cleaning up the mess we know as the Great Depression.

continued

> 'Now, I don't know what name some historian is going to have for the 1980s, but the 1980s will go down in economic history as the equivalent of Tulip Mania. People will look back and say, "How could any sane, sensible human being ever have done it?" We don't know the name, but we do know the symbol that will be in all the history books 100 years from now: Canary Wharf on the Isle of Dogs in London. Twelve billion dollars' worth of construction which is now estimated to have a market value of half a billion and the only way to get to it is swim the River Thames!
>
> 'Think about that. You construct twelve billion dollars' worth of building in a place with no transportation. Or another example: the Japanese built a hotel in Hawaii that was so expensive that, if they rented every single room, every night, all year long for $US2000 they would just break even. Think about that.'

Drucker shocked some delegates at that forum when he forecast that leisure – the super growth market of the 1960s and 1970s, as more and more people worked less and less for more money – was not going to get any bigger. 'It is most unlikely in the developed countries that leisure will grow.' He suggested that in countries like Germany workers would be forced to work harder and put in more productive hours 'if Germany is to remain competitive. Elsewhere, in Japan the hours will still go down but not much and in the USA they are already going up. So leisure is probably at its peak or already past it.'

In healthcare, Drucker talked of an industry racked by crisis that, 'because the healthcare expense has become so big a part it is going to be regulated every place, going to be restrained, going to be rationed.'

In finance Drucker was bullish. But he forecast a very different financial world from the traditional banking house. Pointing out that the old-style bank 'makes its money by not paying enough for its deposits and by overcharging its borrowers' he emphasized that, 'this is no longer possible. There is no country in the world – not even Japan – where people are willing to let the bank have their money without getting an adequate return.' And he argued that there is a new customer out there who will make finance one of the key growth industries of the next ten years, 'except that the customer is totally different from what most financial institutions see in their mind's-eye.'

'Everyone is a customer for investment products,' said Drucker. 'They know, or at least they begin to realize, that they may live to be 90 and may outlive their financial resources. They know now, or at least begin to understand, that their pensions and social security are not quite as solid – because of inflation and the enormous deficit that all developed countries run – and that will force, sooner or later, pretty sharp cuts in social services. So the older people need investment products and are rapidly becoming the best customers.'

An ageing, rich, demanding population is emerging to dominate the mature markets.

This greying population is going to begin to drive much of the way all of us will look at – certainly – the mature markets. As the group with the most money, as the group whose experience in purchasing has a long history, as a group who expect to get what they want and won't settle for less, keeping these customers satisfied will be a major challenge.

As former Dean of MIT's Sloan School, Lester Thurow repeatedly states, 'There are sharp shifts in who has, and who has not, money to spend – a fundamental change in the distribution of wealth. What you should consider is that the new consumer is seventy-years-old and walks with a cane.'

And as we get closer to 2010 – in the developed world at least – those ageing 'grey-panthers' increase in number, spinning off thousands of new products and services.

Back to Drucker and his vision of the global markets of the future. His top tip for tomorrow is education. But education geared to the new technologies. That he suggests 'may be the biggest market of them all – the unlimited appetite for access to the world.'

Coupled to the technological revolutions, this will change the face of global infrastructure projects. ('China is already the

> **Don't forget the developing world**
>
> Although this book is essentially about the modern organization as exemplified by those in the West and to some extent Japan and the new tigers, Paul Tiffany, of the Wharton School urges us not to forget that we make up a very small part of the total global population and land area, even if we do tend to dominate it.
>
> As he says, 'So much of modern management seems oblivious to what is going on elsewhere.' And he raises the hope that we will not just become global players in the easy parts of the world, but we will look for opportunity and business development possibilities in those places that are not as financially rewarding or welcoming. 'Managers of global companies are going to have to expand their horizons – after all, you can't really watch 70 percent of the world in turmoil and not think that it won't affect you.
>
> 'We talk all the time about a tiny corner of what the world is about, our challenge is to make future managers more aware of the other parts and do something about that.'

biggest market for telecommunications, but they are not going to string wires. They are moving to mobile phones, cellular phones, satellites. They are going to leap-frog the developed world.') These are the areas that Drucker in his wisdom is betting on, on past performance, we can probably bet alongside him.

If you are sitting as a manager or an owner, wondering what on earth you are going to do to reap the benefits of tomorrow while keeping the roof from falling in, Peter Drucker has the following advice. 'Look in your own businesses at the implications of all this. How do you fit into a world in which the big consumer demands are for continuing education, which needs a lot of material stuff, for new kinds of finance, for access to the world in all sorts of ways, whether it's education, technology, software, movies or training films.'

And possibly the ultimate advice for the global executive, 'How can I fit all these things into my own business? How would I set the strategy? How can I convert it into an opportunity? How do I make my business fit the rapidly changing world demand patterns?'

To recognize that going global does not come easy, let us close with a hard-nosed comment from John Humble, 'Make no mistake, global competition *is* a life or death struggle. There is no place in any organization for those who do not have a fierce commitment to winning.'

So, it is going to be a tough game out there in the run-up to the next millennium. Competition will be hard, but those best equipped to win may well not be those that we would have bet on just a few short years ago – the giant corporations.

The challenge for the giants will be to trim themselves or break themselves apart sufficiently to take on all-comers in new market battles. Whether senior managers will have the courage to take the axe to the giants they have built with so much care remains to be seen. The most likely scenario is that some will and some will not. Those that reshape and restructure in time will survive and prosper – those that don't will decay and die.

But it isn't just the industry giants who have to become fleet footed. Even those of us in the medium-sized firms will have to be more flexible and we will need a lot of skills to maintain all the advantages without too many of the downsides?

If we can create that balance – that very fine balance – between keeping the customers coming and keeping the organization fighting fit, then we will have succeeded in creating a corporation that meets both success criteria. Keeping that balance over many years is an achievement few people ever succeed in making.

What to watch for

- There aren't any centres anymore. Competition can come from anywhere. But so can opportunities. So what are you doing? Are you out there looking for them, or not?
- Asia is the last great bonanza. But it isn't going to be selling coloured glass to the natives that will make your fortune. Well-thought-out campaigns and a deep understanding and appreciation of other customs and cultures is going to win the day. That understanding can start as soon as you want it to.

- Medium-sized companies will win the business battle, through being faster on their feet. The giants are too slow and ponderous, small companies are just that: too small to know enough, too small to have enough knowledge able workers to fully exploit opportunities. Polish up your resumé and make tracks to a medium-sized company.
- As leisure time levels out, and as some of us increase the work percentage of our lives, so the leisure industry will peak. New financial needs from an ageing population will create new banking and investment services.
- Above all a seeking of knowledge and an urge to travel the information highways will create huge new business opportunities. Will your company take advantage of these developments? Will you be employable in these new industries? The time for checking that out is now, not in ten years' time.

3

Creating the organization of the next millennium

> In the new competitive environment, companies are less and less in a position to carry passengers. There is a growing sense that people who have worked for thirty years in the same firm are too set in their ways, too parochial in their culture. Life on the inside of a company will increasingly become the preserve of the few and the young.
>
> Martin Jacques, *The Sunday Times,* June 1994

> A career is a job that has gone on too long.
>
> *Anonymous*

> In a fight between you and the world, I'd bet on the world.
>
> *Franz Kafka*

We are all supposed to know that the organization is in dire straits. Action is needed now for both individual managers and the organizations they work in to be in shape for 2010 and the rest of the new century. The question is: are your top management actually doing anything about it? More important, if they are bent on making change, are they just tinkering with a tired, old engine, trying a few tweaks to, hopefully, improve performance, or have they actually thought through what needs to be done?

Look inside the company you work for or, if you are part of top management, see honestly how you and your colleagues measure up by asking yourself this: is the top management putting a plan together that cuts costs, cuts people and cuts inventory, because they read in a magazine that's what the competition is doing? Are they into quality improvement, innovation and new marketing ideas because everyone's doing it? Is business-trend fever taking over the organization?

In too many corporations all around the world, rational, intelligent senior managers – and an army of advisers – are doing just that. Cut a little here, put a tuck in here, a stitch or two there and hey presto, you are out promenading in your new corporate clothes.

But, unless top management has seriously thought through the ongoing implications of their actions, those new clothes are going to give at the seams very soon. In extreme circumstances, the organization will find itself naked and exposed, just like the emperor who believed in the flattery of his advisers.

What all managers must understand is that radical change is not a one time event, it is an ongoing process. One that never stops. And none of us should enter into the process without having a good idea of where it is supposed to take us.

Widely acclaimed as the man who has created the re-engineering phenomenon and the co-author of *Re-engineering the Corporation*, James Champy says, 'When companies radically change the way work is performed, only half the job has been done. The remaining challenge may turn out to be more difficult: redesigning underlying management processes.'

A fundamental transformation

In other words it is not enough to see your organization in trouble and chop off the bits that don't work and scale down a few departments – although that might be a part of the process. As Champy himself says, after the first surgery is over, 'executives must fundamentally transform orthodox management models, mind-sets and values from those oriented toward command and control to those that promote and lead an enabled environment.'

 Re-engineering is *not* a project. It is a process that *does not stop!*

Michael Winston, a senior executive at Motorola makes it clear that taking on the idea of re-engineering as a new management cure-it-all, just won't work. 'Reorganization alone will not fix your business. Re-engineering, benchmarking, core process redesign will *not* fix your business. Reason? They are all programmes and the trouble is that all of these, in most people's eyes, have a beginning a middle and an end. Re-engineering – or whatever you want to call it – is a process that does not stop.'

That is why many corporations are still getting the reorganization they need now – to survive into the next millennium – so badly wrong. Not because they are failing to make the deep cuts required, but because they are missing the second page of the new corporate age instruction manual.

And the strange part, about this failure to enact the second part of the equation, is that they are missing out on the positive aspects of the manager's job – not the cuts but the creation.

To stand any chance of surviving into the twenty-first century, companies have to take that second step – and soon. INSEAD's Professor of Strategy and Management, Sumatra Ghoshal says that 'too many companies have concentrated on 50 percent reduction in inventory, 40 percent reduction in capital, 40 percent reduction in people. This is the part that managers hate.'

But he believes that dramatic performance improvement – which after all is what it is all about – is not possible without doing the things that managers really like – and what they should be getting paid for – the creation and the pursuit of opportunities.

To go to that second stage top management need to change from being what Ghoshal calls 'guardians of structure to architects of progress'.

But the highly respected management commentator, Henry Mintzberg is deeply concerned that management isn't getting it right, and brutal change is having a knock-on effect. Mintzberg says that 'there is a mindlessness in today's management. If delayering is so wonderful why weren't we doing it in 1980?'

He's right. Unfortunately, for most of us those BFOs (blinding flashes of the obvious) just weren't there in 1980 for, our then, top managers to see. Nothing succeeds like hindsight.

Mintzberg brutally calls it, 'culling by numbers, that', he says 'is deeply upsetting and seems to be adopted mindlessly.'

He asks, 'How can you maintain a change process when the key actors have left? How do you keep the others devoted?'

This is the one part that isn't going to be at all easy. It is also the part that many managers are going to have to be retrained to do anything like an effective job. Furthermore, they will have to learn to take into account in their decision the trilogy of shareholders, employees and customers. Only if all of these groups benefit can the organization be healthy in the longer term. Too often, in the heat of crisis, management panders to shareholder concerns and focuses on short-term profit, when they should be concerned about their customers and their employees. In tomorrow's world creating this balance will be ever more critical. As Mintzberg hints, making your shareholders and customers happy is a short-term gain if your employees (the core of the intellectual capital your organization depends on) walk out of the door.

So getting an effective balance between the three pillars of the organization – the three groups of stakeholders – is going to become one of the main challenges for managers of the twenty-first century. That is also the challenge of today to get any organization re-launched for tomorrow.

Jim Champy has at least part of the answer to Mintzberg's concerns. 'With fewer managerial jobs and levels to aspire to, managers will have a big challenge in motivating the higher performers. The first part of the answer is to disconnect managerial positions from compensation.' Meaning that you can't reward them in the same way as the rest of the staff. And, it has already become obvious that the high flyers don't want to be regarded as the same. Want to keep them? Think of new ways to reward them – quickly.

Champy goes on to point out that, 'Some of an organization's highest and most valued performers should be paid commensurate with their contribution – not their rank. In fact you don't want many of them taking on management jobs.'

 The old motivators don't work anymore. Sit down and ask yourself 'how can I get my people excited again about our business?'

'Second, with all this industry and process re-invention going on, your employees will be depending more than ever on management to lead them through all the confusion. If you want to keep them, your high performers will have to get excited by your purpose for the business – that is your articulation of how the organization is going to fit in a fast changing marketplace. They'll have to be motivated by the new business you're moving to. And you'll have to compensate them for work well done. The old motivators of promotions and power will go away.'

Keen observer of business metamorphosis and author of *Managing on the Edge*, Richard Pascale sees these flatter organizations requiring fewer and fewer managers. 'I don't think we'll need no management at all, but I think the role of what technology effectively does is to substitute the traditional role of management. When you empower people and have them work on self managed teams a lot of what managers have historically done goes away. So you don't need those levels.'

Empowerment: not a fad

And in case anyone thinks otherwise, Pascale adds, 'empowerment is not a fad, it is something that is going to grow. Because it is fundamental to the transformations that are now taking place and it goes hand in hand with both what technology enables us to do and what the needs of the competitive environment require in terms of response time.'

N. Venkatraman of Boston University's Business School tells managers to think of the change like this, 'Take the task for which you are a manager. Take the domain for which you presently have management responsibilities. If you were a new entrant into that market-place today and if you had to design an organization from scratch to compete against your organization, would that organization be anything like what you are managing now? And if the answer is "no", that is the reference point that you have to think about.'

Radically changing the way the organization works isn't going to be easy for anyone, but it is beginning to be seen as the only real way to play the business game of the future. What this means in essence is that it isn't just the hierarchies that flatten, but the jobs change as well. If you are in a staff job today (see box on HR, page 48) you had better find a way of becoming a specialist making a measurable and relevant contribution. Otherwise, the change machine that is already up and running is going to roll right over you.

Innovate, innovate, innovate

Michael Porter, the man who has done more to make us think about competition than anyone else, sees that one of the prime keys to organizational effectiveness over the next fifteen years is the ability of the companies we work for to innovate.

Without that ability inherent in our structures, our businesses are doomed to falter and stall somewhere on that route to 2010.

Porter says, 'The USA is world-class in software. Not because we are efficient, but because we are innovative, because we continue to pump out new and better products at an incredible rate in that particular business compared to anywhere else on this globe.'

He gives another example. 'The Japanese are winning in consumer electronics, not because they are efficient, but they can beat the Koreans and the Taiwanese because they are innovative, they keep improving product features, they keep on improving product quality, they keep on improving what the products do – they make them more compact, more multi-functional. That is what creates advantage and it's not just innovation in science, it's innovation in everything. It is how you perform service, it is how you do sales, it is how you position your product in the market. Innovation must be seen broadly.'

 Winners anticipate world market trends ... they don't follow them.

Porter concludes, 'If you sit still at any one place, you're dead. Because some other country or company with cheaper wages or some other location with even hungrier people will come and take the business away from you. If you are a stationary target for very long information and technology flows so freely that it is going to diffuse very rapidly. The only way to be competitive is to progress. To be a world-class company you not only have to be innovative, but be innovative in ways that are valued not only in your own country but elsewhere. The world leaders are usually the ones who can improve their products in directions that really anticipate world market trends rather than follow them.'

The market-driven enterprise

As marketing's top thinker, Philip Kotler is certain that we have already moved well on our way to an organization driven by processes not functions. 'I think that marketing will be handled by much more of a team. I'm convinced that marketing doesn't work when it is a set of often conflicting specialities (research, sales, advertising, promotion and so forth). It works best when cemented into a team that sets its sights on a target.'

And as many think that marketing won the organizational war hands down, in that all the efforts of today's and tomorrow's corporation will be towards getting the product or service right for the customer, marketing isn't going to be the same either. With the entire organization essentially marketing-driven, the discipline will become the all pervasive operational base.

Kotler's view is reinforced by INSEAD's Professor of Marketing, Jean-Claude Larréché, 'Of course I believe that marketing is and will remain the drive of the business organization. How could it not be, as the client is in the end the real leader of a business entity? However, marketing is going through a transformation that will make it look very different by 2010. I would see manufacturing, distribution and logistics being amalgamated into a separate support function, while marketing, innovation and human resources would be the three pillars of the central organization with finance as a controlling function reporting directly to the board of the corporation.'

Then of course you can take former Harvard professor Tom Bonoma's view that, 'The existence of marketing is as the abject failure of management. Because all representatives of the organization should have that function.'

All this would seem to indicate that you need a top management that knows marketing inside out. That view has been supported by research done at the University of Columbia, which combined with executive search consultants, Korn Ferry to produce a study on chief executives in the year 2000. Interviewed at the time for a Management Centre Europe report on new management ideas, Donald Hambrick, who led the study, said, 'At Columbia we have been examining the whole question of functional background. One of our conclusions is that there is some disadvantage in companies being run by people from what we call the 'peripheral' functional areas –

Wanted: more internationalism

One of the key issues that almost every expert has on his or her check list for the future is the ability to be global in scope, not just in their products and markets they serve, but in the people who will work in the organization. As Liam Fahey suggested, a Japanese company headed by non-Japanese and located in Dusseldorf. Additionally, successful global corporations of the next century are supposed to be culturally diverse, with a mix of nationalities at the top, otherwise how can they ever understand the nuances and needs of their markets.

Sadly, recent research shows that this is not the case. A recent research study involving 700 European managers by Management Centre Europe showed that companies are doing very little in real terms to come to grips with the multinational world they live in.

Although the vast majority feel that it is vital for the future that their organization becomes more international at top management level, few could admit that this was either happening or planned for.

What the survey – 'How International are You and Your Company?' clearly proved was that there was plenty of talk, plenty of discussion, plenty of advice, but precious little positive action.

Highlights from the research make gloomy reading:

- Asked if the company they work for 'regards itself as international in outlook', eight out of ten respondents said 'yes'.
- Asked if they 'personally consider themselves to be an international manager,' 65 percent said 'yes'.
- Asked if they thought that 'to ensure growth and survival, companies will need a mixture of different nationalities at top level in corporate headquarters,' 86 percent said 'yes'.

BUT

- Asked if there are 'enough foreign nationals (at any level) in your corporate headquarters', six out of ten said 'no'.
- Asked how many of the main board directors at world headquarters (one-third of those polled worked for US corporations), were foreign nationals just 12 percent reported between 1 and 10 percent. Only 5 percent of respondents said it was between 11 and 20 percent.

continued

(from previous page)
- Asked if there was a policy 'in your company' for the recruitment and promotion of foreign nationals to top management positions, seven out of ten managers said 'no'.
- Asked if, as their company did not have foreign nationals today, was there 'a policy to have them in the future', just 6 percent could say 'yes, definitely'.

What this survey shows in quite dramatic figures, is that while the management commentators and consultants are talking of the absolute necessity of having a globally mixed top management team, no notice is being take of this whatsoever at grass roots level, even though they state that they wish they were doing something about it.

Indeed, according to the Management Centre Europe survey, the three greatest barriers cited in the poll to a diversified mix of nationalities were:

Differing management styles	45 per cent
Misconceptions about other nationalities	29 per cent
Historical animosities	13 per cent

Perhaps now we can understand, in part at least, why companies have so much trouble realizing their global ambitions.

The worst culprits – the most nationalistically inclined – are most certainly European firms. This lack of international attitude was addressed at a 1994 senior executive briefing, by Peter Drucker, who pointed out that the most 'European' companies were, in fact, from the USA and Japan. But he added, 'the French and Italians have barely tackled it and the English don't know the issue is there. It is easier as a European to build a business in the USA than Europe.'

One of the major barriers to getting a nationality mix is that few of the top management really have had any transnational business experience. A European marketing manager said in the survey, 'It's amazing how few top managers have worked in another European country, more have worked in the USA' For many managers, experience of other European countries is based on vacations, not doing business.

Peter Drucker says that 'if you decide to go European, within five years a non-national will have to be in your top management, if only to symbolically prove that you are no longer a national company.

continued

He and others also stress that a failure to take a European route – let alone a global route – will cut the organization off from a major pool of talent. And as talent gets scarce, you will want to be able to attract the best, not just a Belgian, because you are a Belgian company. If you don't it will be like having an invisible sign up that proclaims 'foreigners not wanted'.

Taking the going global needs further, Management Centre Europe's poll asked managers the question, if they had foreigners working in their headquarters, where did they come from? American, British, French and German dominated, with no one from others parts of the world even mentioned.

Asked what nationalities they would prefer to work with the Europeans said North Americans, the North Americans said European, and the Japanese said Japanese, with other Asians a second choice. On these results alone, from a corporate culture standpoint, a bi-polar world could well be on the way.

Former Dean of MIT's Sloan School of Management, Lester Thurow thinks that Japan's inability to let foreigners into corporations could 'make them lose out, as their culture won't make it happen, while it will be easier for countries like the USA and the UK to recruit not just talented people, but talented foreigners.'

Finally, the 700 managers were asked which country was the 'symbol of a nation with the most global approach to business?' Twenty-four percent said Japan, ahead of the USA with 23 percent, the Dutch with 13 percent and the British with 8 percent. On the basis of the failure of most of our corporations to tackle the nationality mix in any effective way the results probably owe more to the marketing power of Toyota and Sony and the advertising budgets of Coca-Cola and Marlboro than anything else.

---

finance, law and administration – as opposed to core functions like R&D, sales and marketing and operations.'

Hambrick concluded by discussing the harm that peripheral function leaders often do. 'They achieve some quick improvements – such as cleaning up the balance sheet, cutting costs and rationalizing operations – but the company may be left in unhealthy condition and, strategically, may even be set on the road to disaster.'

That's exactly what Jim Champy, Sumantra Ghoshal, Richard Pascal and other leaders of the organizational revolution are worried about if companies think they have achieved the necessary change with a few quick fixes.

What's the purpose of your business?

Because everyone – even the best and brightest – is in danger of getting it wrong if they don't keep thinking future, future, future, innovate, innovate, innovate, they also need to make sure they see the re-engineering process as just that: a process which flows and continues as an ongoing way of being in business.

As Jim Champy says, 'If you haven't answered the question about purpose you increasingly run the risk of re-engineering a process in an obsolete business.' Or as Michael Porter stresses in the Insight, page 39, you can be doing things quite efficiently but it's no good if it's irrelevant to today's market.

Purpose means that you have to 'show and tell' what your plans are. Make it good and make it simple, because after all they have been through in the last half decade, the audience might just be a tiny bit cynical.

Champy observes, 'In addition, the articulation of purpose is critical for mobilizing the organization. It gets your people off and running and responds to their interests and fears about where the company is heading.'

Most people – stressed with the processes, not to mention the agonies of change – don't bother to tell what's going on. But you have to make time for this – it's critical.

To make it abundantly clear that you cannot stop half-way in the change process, Champy stresses, 'The question about process is two-fold. What new operational processes are needed and what new management processes do we need to run those new operational processes, such as mobilizing, enabling, defining, measuring and communicating?'

 The cut, cut, cut manager will be replaced, with someone who can build and develop for the future.

But, as has already been suggested, this also raises the issue that the man who can cut, cut, cut to get to the desired leanness and meanness is not the man – or woman – to sail the new ship into the future. Wharton professor George Day says, 'The residue of re-engineering may mean that we have processes but the question will be, how do we innovate inside these systems? The cost-cutting manager has driven productivity, but what happens then?'

And he makes the telling point that in the aftermath of part one of the re-engineering process, 'growth and innovation will become a much higher priority and this will require a much different manager. The cost-cutter cannot do this!'

If, as Donald Hambrick's research suggested, you have a chief executive from the finance discipline, he may be OK when you really have to do some serious tearing down of traditional business areas that are no longer valid. But in building a winning organization for the future, he is not necessarily going to be the one to motivate and coach a dynamic, innovative team.

Hambrick's research also threw up another worry. Who chooses the chief executive?

'If the chief executive (CEO) has chosen his successor himself,' warns Hambrick, 'there is at least some of his old, unwanted mind-set being passed on.'

That is why he believes that 'the succession decision should be taken away from the CEO. The idea of one-on-one tutelage – or the passing of the baton as it is often seen – has a certain merit. But only if it doesn't imply that the outgoing CEO has done the selection. That clearly raises the risk of cloning.'

One of the reasons that we should all consider when changing our CEO, or giving him something else to do when the first, quick and dirty part is over – usually associated with downsizing and chopping much loved limbs from the corporate tree – is that the structure of organizations – without the command and control systems of before – won't be a place that is remotely recognizable.

As Liam Fahey points out the new-age firm is going to take some getting used to. Like moving into a new house. 'We are talking about a federated organization, disseminating ideas and knowledge. The new model is a federation of alliances that do not control all their operations – I think every large enterprise is going that way.'

The new general manager

But, Fahey raises an interesting idea about what could happen to all those so-called middle managers who the corporation of tomorrow won't need, because we are living in a world of top management and specialists. 'The real paradox in the world of 2010 is that if you need to have more and more dispersed management knowledge it means that middle managers become general managers doing top management jobs. So top managers will have to change to allow this to happen and you will have an organization that looks like an inverted pyramid.'

So that's where we are going to be in 2010 – the opposite of today. Our twelve level, vertical pyramid of 1990, is gradually turning on its axis 180 degrees, where the point looks down and it is only three or five levels deep.

Easy enough to visualize. Not that easy to practise.

Therefore what do the brightest and the best think of the organization of tomorrow? Do we have any examples or ideas of what it will look like?

Law firm, orchestra, or what?

There's an old joke ascribed to a management guru which suggests that if the corporation of the future is flat, then the obvious model would be a law firm. The punch line is that it would never work as the executives would spend their time suing their clients!

Investigate your law firm, consultancy, even your local orchestra. Can you make your organization look like that?

Jokes apart, law firms, consulting firms, opera companies and orchestras have all been touted as the next shape of the business organization. For as more and more people work in teams, work as specialists, sell their knowledge to the highest bidder, structures never stand still.

The ever aware Peter Drucker fancies the symphony orchestra or the opera as an idea. 'There is no management between the conductor and the individual player. Another is the opera, where there is no management layer between the diverse cast: orchestra, singers, chorals and the conductor.' The rewards for this type of organization come in the responsibility, the demands on the individual and the getting and keeping of the role. The other is money. If, like an opera, you know who is performing it is easy to reward the right people.

Liam Fahey reckons that 'the consulting firm might point the way' and it might be that 'business can learn from institutions like the UN and NATO'.

Richard Pascale says that, 'maybe the way to look is at the law firm, or the way a consulting firm or some investment banks work, where you don't have a lot of hierarchy and people basically work on one project after another. Rank is not signified by the size of their offices or the importance of their title, it comes from having larger and larger responsibilities and growing professionally in their confidence over a lifetime.'

George Day suggests that as the whole process will become team driven there will be 'short lives and long lives. Short-term, like a management consultancy and long-term like order processing.' But his worry is that we must find where the true skill bases of our organizations lie, 'where is the knowledge for these processes. If we don't do this thoroughly it will be difficult, perhaps impossible to let go of the notion of functions. And that will get us back to the old command control model.'

Interestingly enough, T.W. Kang, author of *Gaishi, the Foreign Company in Japan*, points out that this 180 degree roll we are supposed to be undergoing will move at a slower pace in Asia. Indicating that if the West gets moving now, this might be a an opportunity to get an advantage over Japan and other Asian economies.

Says Kang, 'The tendency will be towards a flatter organization, but Asian firms are more likely to follow in that direction at a slower pace because of strong Confucian influences regarding hierarchy, status consciousness and so on.'

Kang is heading toward Liam Fahey's idea of the remainder of middle managers finding themselves at the top of the inverted pyramid as general managers in far flung parts of the corporate empire. 'Multi-divisional companies will, to a much

Goodbye human resources?

One area that stands to get hit harder than most in the organizational changes impacting the corporation is human resources (HR). Already viewed by many managers as never having really made it as a fully paid-up member of the top management ranks, its relevance as a function in a delayered, seamless process system is more nebulous than ever. About as relevant as the person with the triangle in the orchestra that many say will be the form the flatter organization will take (see main text).

A senior manager recently described the three major moans of HR as, 'If only we were invited to management meetings. If only we were asked for our opinion. If only we had more status and credibility.' And he went on to suggest that HR's crisis was like that of 'a blind man trying to describe what an elephant looks like while holding only the trunk.'

To business strategy expert Mark Thomas, explanations like that sound the death knell of HR – and any other staff functions that don't directly contribute to the business. 'HR should consider re-branding itself "performance support". The function must be totally centred on providing real business support if it is to survive. It should focus on harnessing the latest advances in technology to provide managers with real tools to exploit the performance of their people.'

Warming to the subject he goes on, 'At the moment, too many functions are still expensive administrative functions. These functions will not survive. The technology to replace these low-level functions is already here. It is only a matter of time before the technology really attacks the higher value-added functions of HR and generates innovative solutions to performance management, monitoring and development.'

Confirmation for Thomas's beliefs comes from a senior human resources manager, 'if HR doesn't think business it will always be brought in at the tail-end of decisions. Also younger managers have no confidence in an administrative HR function in which political game-playing is big, since this is the only means left for HR to play some kind of role in the company. The future of HR may well be with the line manager – with high calibre business managers taking over the HR role and with people consultants (not HR, not personnel) among line managers.'

continued

The pressure on today's HR managers to transform themselves to something that is part of the fast paced firm of the future is something they must recognize. Seen by many as never getting higher than an upper middle management function, and with no middle managers in future corporate scenarios, they have to become hands-on specialists or move over and let someone else – more attuned to the needs of the twenty-first century corporation – take over.

> HR managers *must* implement programmes that add bottom-line value to the business ... otherwise you don't need them.

Guy Mollett, a management development specialist at Volkswagen, stresses this urgency for HR to take a positive business role. 'The role of HR executives will be to help develop, support and implement overall company strategies. They must start implementing do-able things and stop developing major schemes and grand bureaucratic concepts that never fly.'

This lack of real future vision to do things that truly support the business – that is turning HR into the first corporate casualty of the reorganization wars – is a view supported by Mark Thomas. 'All too often the HR function has engrossed itself in developing esoteric initiatives which prove overly complex and at worst irrelevant to the needs of the organization.'

And in getting HR to face up to the drama of the new organization, Thomas goes further, 'I would also abolish words such as "careers" and "jobs". As organizations are beginning to realize, the future is about flexibility and to that extent "role" is a far better word to use. Careers with one employer are now a thing of the past and we need to promote new and more radical messages to staff. Indeed, I would want to be certain that in all areas HR is promoting the future organization and not perpetuating the past by its continued use of outmoded concepts and words.'

It would seem on past performance that some HR professionals will find a new, successful 'role' for themselves. Others unable to function in the flatter organizations of tomorrow, where you are only as valuable as your specialized contribution, will not.

greater degree, have division headquarters located in competence centres around the world instead of having one corporate headquarters location.' Which also lends some support to that theory that the best of today's middle management *cadre* will find themselves as *de facto* top managers, running an independent, functional subsidiary.

However, before everyone gets too excited, let us not forget that there are an awful lot of middle managers in the world – even today. There are not that many positions for mini-general managers. So anyone thinking of this development being a way out – an escape route – for the beleaguered middle manger should think again.

However, almost unanimously the world's top business thinkers and advisers are in no doubt that we have come past the point of no return in terms of organizational change. You can literally hear the changes happening all around you.

And those changes are going to go on for some time yet.

Put another way, we are already on the roller-coaster, but we are still climbing to the vertical point where the excitement really begins. When we get to the top, there will be little time to admire the view, we will all be too busy holding on as we slide around a few new organizational curves.

What the descent after the climb will look like, we are still trying to work out. No one is quite sure what our organization of tomorrow is actually going to look like. Richard Pascale, is as puzzled as the rest of us.

In an honest discussion, and picking up on his earlier statements, Richard Pascale made this point about the job satisfaction the experts think we'll all get when we are part of the self-motivated, totally empowered team.

'You know Maslow said that people wanted not only physical security but they also want self-esteem – which might be status; I mean to do with job titles and office sizes and self actualization, which might be banking on a new psychological contract that gives a lot of self actualization and not a lot else.

'Is that viable? I'm not sure. To attack my earlier example that law firms, consulting firms and investment banks are perhaps models of the future, they are very flat and they do all the things I described earlier, but they also pay people a great deal when they are at a senior level. So there are huge amounts of financial remuneration available in those kind of firms. A Jack Welch or a General Electric couldn't create a system inside most of his businesses that could afford to pay people for what they were not getting in other ways, through their "parking lot" perks. And that is the problem, that I don't think we have answers for – a big question.'

The other issue that needs to be aired is that much of the examples of empowered, highly motivated teams are based on research and ideas coming out of the USA, because that is where 99 percent of all the management gurus come from – and it is their articles, books and lectures that colour the way we perceive our own organizations should be moving.

Be careful with the culture

But, as organizations take on these changes, we must all be mindful that some cultures – and not half-way down the Amazon either – don't take kindly to empowerment or even the dismantling of the structures they feel safe and protected inside. So, while change is necessary, how it is introduced, how it is explained is just as important as the actual mechanics.

Richard Hill, a Brussels-based business commentator and self-styled Euro-anthropologist, and author of *We Europeans*, comments on the disastrous experiences companies with a matrix management organization have had in places like Italy, Portugal and Spain. 'Southern European's cannot cope with conflicting instructions, they cannot work that way. They need one boss who tells them what to do.' Indeed proud Spaniards have been known to walk off the job if they are asked to do something they consider demeaning or below their status. So, before introducing any sweeping changes, think through how the news will be received in the different 'culture pockets' around the business. Then adapt your message of what you are doing and when it is happening to meet local needs.

Think global, act local, doesn't just apply to the customers – it applies to your own organization as well.

 It isn't enough to be clever with your customers and make them feel you understand them ... thinking global and acting local applies to the people *inside* your company as well.

Outsource, but don't give away your secrets

One of the set pieces for revitalizing your organization is outsourcing – at least it is if you get it right. Business watchers like Peter Drucker and Michael Porter say that the reason medium-sized companies are the likely winners in the next century is that they won't be carrying so much baggage around with them, having outsourced all the bits and pieces they just don't need to have under their everyday control.

In fact a Coopers and Lybrand survey shows that the three top reasons for outsourcing are:

- outsiders are more efficient
- you can focus on your own products
- you save costs on benefits

All good reasons for hiving off unproductive and cost-creating parts of the business. Increasingly this means paring down the company to the bare bones, allowing managers to concentrate on managing the parts that really perform.

Says Lou Stern a professor of marketing at Northwestern University, 'To a large extent everyone wants a turnkey solution. They don't want to assemble by themselves, they want someone to take over the function and that's the role of outsourcing and facility management.'

Stern notes that as we move into the next century, 'more and more companies will become networked, modular corporations. Nike designs and markets running shoes, but someone else does the rest.' And he adds, 'so inter-organizational management becomes a critical advantage.'

 What processes *must* you own inside your company, and what you can do without and outsource?

But outsourcing must be seen as another part of the change process, not just having former pieces of the business done by someone else, because they do it for less. Says N. Vekatraman of Boston University's School of Management, 'We are increasingly asking the question, "what processes should I own inside the organization?" Do we need to have

continued

accounts payable inside, when the best accounts payable provided by AT&T, Universal Card or American Express or anybody else can process a cheque at a fraction of the cost of what we can achieve inside the organization.'

He says that organizations have to ask the question, '"How much does it cost to process a cheque and what is the best class process parameter for processing a cheque?" If that is not in your organization, doesn't it make sense for you to have an alliance or a relationship with somebody else who can provide that capability?'

However, there is a downside to all this. Having seen companies over eager to outsource get it very badly wrong, consultant and author John Humble warns against outsourcing at any price. 'Outsourcing is a great idea when it is done well, but there are, sadly, a growing number of companies who find they have outsourced what they ultimately discover is their core competence.'

And Richard Pascale points out that, particularly with today's financial pressures and the need to make the results look good, outsourcing is not necessarily done as a move to rid the corporation of work that can be accomplished better elsewhere. It can and is being used for other, more cosmetic purposes. 'More and more outsourcing today is really a Trojan horse for off balance sheet financing. A lot of outsourcing today is in effect really a company getting cash for assets that have not been capitalized.'

Hill adds, 'attempts to introduce matrix management to German companies has also met with strong resistance and incomprehension. There's also a problem with empowerment in some European countries. That's something that American firms, most of all, need to learn, people in some cultures just don't want to be empowered.'

In another example, he says that management by objectives and its countless derivatives, 'will never work in a place like Spain. The MBO system rewards on the basis of performance measurement – the Spanish just don't like being checked up on.'

Making technology count

Re-engineering's high priest, Jim Champy is keen to make it clear that much of what drives the impetus for a mega-change in the way our corporation's operate, are the new technologies.

Using technology

To make sure that we make effective use of the new technologies as they become available, he advises all of us to, 'ask what business you really should be in. What's this business for? That question has become more important because our markets are changing so rapidly. Technology – particularly information technology – is driving this. You now must continuously re-examine your product and service offerings against your opportunities and what your customers demand. You must re-examine the purpose of your organization.

'If you are a newspaper publisher, you must ask yourself whether your fundamental purpose is to print news on paper and distribute it through news-stands, racks and kids – especially with the coming of the information superhighway. The newspaper's fundamental purpose is to provide news and related information to an audience that advertisers want to reach. How you provide that news may change. Most executives are not asking questions about the fundamental purposes of their enterprises.'

Long-term goals for organizations

Trying to force the attention of hard-worked executives to the future has been a long-term goal of Gary Hamel of the London Business School and C.K. Prahalad of the University of Michigan.

In their latest, best-selling business book *Competing for the Future*, they provide eight questions for managers to answer, to see if they are really focused on the future of their organizations.

Another person raises an eyebrow in some doubt about whether devolution and empowerment will be the total success everyone talks of today. Nick Winkfield, Director of International Operations at market research firm, MORI and a leading expert on organizational attitudes, says, 'Central functions such as strategic planning have already largely disappeared, coordination between business units and functions has been sacrificed in favour of devolution and empowerment – but the possible downsides of all this have yet to become visible – by the time it does it will be too late to change quickly.

'Therefore, the key skills for the year 2010 will be speed and a willingness to fly by the seat of the pants. But there will be an emerging role for "business integrators" who will plan strategies and coordinate their implementation, to bring under control the centrifugal forces of devolution and empowerment which will, by then, have made most large organizations unmanageable.'

Embrace constructive tension

Richard Pascale can relate to Winkfield's point of view. 'I believe very strongly that one of the shifts in our paradigm is to be one where we embrace constructive tension. The most successful organizations – that seem to stay successful over time – will be able to embrace the contradiction of having very rigid systems and values in some areas and allowing a lot of independent and autonomous behaviour in others. I think Intel, Nordstrom, Goldman-Sachs and JP Morgan are great examples of that.'

Whatever the ultimate scenario, one thing the manager of tomorrow is going to want is something to hold onto, and the new organization may or may not be able to offer them that. As the traditional icons of the West (the church, the family, education and the law) that have lasted for practically the whole of this millennium vanish, people need something to replace them.

For those who have had the trauma of redundancy, there is hope that they will find a new organization that they can belong to. For those left behind, the 180 degree turn that they are involved in will either bring a sort of kaleidoscopic stability – if the organization knows how to create a new sense of purpose – or they will slowly move to other pastures.

Change is not an option

But let's say it loud and clear. These fundamental changes will not be an option. They are happening out there in the real world right now, and they will continue happening all the way down that long, long road to 2010. Any person, any enterprise, any industry, any country that does not invest in innovation and new skills to fight the future is obsolete. You may say, people in your organization may say 'I don't want to do it that way'. Fine, but go and do something else, because in the world of business tomorrow, if you don't keep investing in yourself, you're dead. And this will also apply to countries that don't help their industrial base prepare for tomorrow and don't understand that the old rules no longer apply. If your country doesn't have an effective and supportive enterprise culture maybe the most innovative thing you can do is to move out to a place where tomorrow's business climate is better understood.

Here is the dilemma: organizations must change. But having changed, having re-engineered their processes, having created a new work method, they must put back that sense of trust that has been smashed, otherwise people – at the end of the day – won't work.

As corporate strategist John Elkins says, 'There isn't much loyalty today because companies don't show much to employees. What we need to ask ourselves is whether in the future loyalty is a tangible asset. We have taken humanity out of the culture of the corporation, it now represents just a place to go to work. I think that company loyalty is going to be a big issue for companies to work on for the next fifteen to twenty years.'

Former Harvard professor Tom Bonoma concurs, 'Most of us spend the majority of our time at work, so today's business is also in a way our house and family. What we have to do is motivate and develop people as if they were relatives, not employees.

'We must equip them to deal with the world when they are no longer in our company.'

The role of the woman manager

In all of this preparation for the future, nothing has been said of the role of the female executive. That is mainly because it is simpler to see an executive as a professional, neither male or female, than to examine these large issues from the point of view of the management sexes.

In the course of the interviews and the discussions for this book, there were very few specific references to women executives. However, several people pointed out that enrolments to business schools in the USA by women was down, and the trend was looking that way. Several others ventured that the news was filtering back down the age brackets that a career in business wasn't necessarily the way to go and there were, other, more rewarding opportunities, professions and careers.

Certainly, looking round major corporations in the USA and Europe – Japan in this respect doesn't count at all – it is still difficult to find women in senior – or next to senior positions.

But with the flattening of our organizations, could that be set to change? With the eventual departure of the current – still extremely male dominated – generation, could we be in for something new?

The best answer to this question comes from Richard Pascale. 'I think in the world we have been describing – the kind of profile we have created – the manager of the future or the person of the future effectively works in teams. Women in Western society are socialized to play that role more effectively than men, so I think women more often than not meet the profile of that future team player and leader than a lot of men do.'

Paul Kahn, now CEO at SafeCard Services and former President and CEO at AT&T Universal Card, says, 'My idea as a manager is that the more you bring the best out in people you create an environment where they want to come to work

 Employees in the successful company of tomorrow will be equipped to like change and *expect* it as well.

every day. It's a question of creating what I call adult management, against most management that is parent to child.'

And he says, 'I want to grow employees so I need a company to grow, I consider a parting of the ways a failure. But I also know I don't owe me to them, I owe me to my company.'

Starting to like change

Brussels-based executive search consultant Wim Noortman suggests that in the new world of the next millennium, management will have to know where to draw the line; where the organization's responsibilities end and the employee's begin. 'We must prepare employees for change in such a way that they start liking change and start to see change as a normal commodity rather than a nerve-racking situation. We have to help all employees understand that only they themselves are responsible for creating, maintaining and enlarging their careers. Companies must provide the tools and systems to enable employees to do so, but that is where it should stop.'

A constantly changing environment has been the environment for Theo Lieven, ever since he and his partner founded computer retailer, Vobis, a decade ago. Now Europe's number one retailer of PCs Vobis got there by 'doing things a little better every day,' and being faster than any of their competitors. With a hard core of tough, entrepreneurial managers that have grown with the organization, Lieven's model might be the organization of 2010 in prototype. Asked what his people do best he says, 'What our people like the most is when there is a competitor making trouble, then we all team up and work out how to defend ourselves.'

And that, thinks Lieven, may be the way for stage two of Vobis, which although already delayered and highly empowered as an organization is constantly reinventing itself. 'When you have a company that has been used to fight every day, perhaps it really needs to fight every day.'

Long an admirer of Hewlett-Packard (which became Lieven's role model for their ability to combine innovation, entrepreneurship and professional management), he says the only thing he didn't like was when they published their 'ten laws of the organization'. It seemed too institutionalized for him.

'All the same,' he muses, 'we might need them some day as well. Perhaps law number one should be "pick someone to fight with everyday" '.

Confronting the problems

Another man who knows a lot about reality is the recently arrived CEO of AT&T Europe, Pier Carlo Falotti, the man who built Digital Equipment's European operations into a giant. Underscoring the need that organizations really do have to get down to the task of change, and that it is a constant process he says, 'Most of us know only too well what our problems are if we look in the mirror and are honest with ourselves. We just don't want to admit it. We tend to feel unconsciously that if no one talks about the problem it will go away. So we just don't confront it.'

Put your faith in interpersonal skills: you'll need all of them.

To make change work, and to foster change what you have to do says Falotti, is, 'come in and say, this is what we are going to do, this is how we are going to change. I know that a percentage are going to be very enthusiastic and positive and say "yes" and get on with it. Another percentage are going to say "now we are facing the problems and perhaps it will be different". Then there will be another percentage who will say, "it will never work" '.

The first two groups will embrace change and use it as an opportunity to grow, it is that final percentage that all managers need to work on to get their motivation and trust.

> **INSIGHT**
>
> **Don't waste talent**
>
> They may have differing views on a lot of things, and be very different personalities, but Peter Drucker and Mike Kami both agree on one thing: far too many companies waste their talented people.
>
> Drucker says, 'We put our high performers onto damage prevention, that's keeping yesterday alive.' Kami adds, 'Don't put your bright people onto the problems, that way all the opportunities are managed by idiots!'

The real shape of the organization of 2010 isn't quite there yet. But several things are clear. It isn't going to look anything like the ones we are working in today. It is going to be run by a hard-nosed, innovative cadre of top managers, but not a series of Genghis Kahn look-alikes. They are going to have to spend a lot more of their time on interpersonal issues, building confidence in the people that work for them, either full-time or as contractors. Support staff will be specialists in their area, constantly growing and adding to their knowledge and will work in multi-functional teams, breaking up when assignments and projects are complete.

There are a lot of tough decisions to be made in the next five years. Hopefully, we will have the leaders to make those tough decisions. What they, and those who work for them, will need as personal attributes is the subject of the next chapter.

What to watch for

- Re-engineering is not the quick fix, magic medicine that many companies think. It is a never-ending process that keeps on going, to 2010 and after. Remember, don't get stuck with only the first part of the re-engineering instruction book – the bit about change – you need the process as well to deal effectively with the future.

> **INSIGHT·INSIGHT·INSIG**
>
> **No too small**
>
> With the suggestion that the day of the giant corporation might be on the wane and the fast, flexible middle-sized corporation is the role model for the future, whatever happened to 'small is beautiful?'
>
> Lou Stern, Professor of Management at Northwestern University has one suggestion. 'For a business graduate, running a small company can be really nickel and dime. There's an awful lot of basic grunt work you have to do. It's not a simple process, it may sound nice, but once you get into it – is it really?'
>
> Additionally, Peter Drucker believes that you need to be of a certain size to take advantage of opportunities and have enough depth of talent to be a really knowledge-based organization.

- The manager's job is to create excitement in the work environment, to put back a sense of place and purpose that too many companies have been missing for too long.
- Marketing won the business battle. Now we are all marketers; at least we are all marketers in the company that is going to see 2010. If you are not in a company that is market-driven, go and find one – soon!
- The fire, fire, fire, chop, chop, chop Arnold Schwarzenegger management era is practically over. There isn't a single manager for all seasons. What is needed now is the re-builder, the visionary to take the company into the future. If Arnie's still hanging around the board room in twelve months' time, you may be in the wrong company at the wrong time.
- The new, flat organization may look like your local orchestra or theatre company: five levels maximum from tip to toe. All playing together on the team, all sharing talents, all knowing who plays the wrong chords. An intensive, intelligent organization for tomorrow.
- With so much change about, there are young managers around today who never knew anything else. So constant

change isn't going to frighten them, it's just part of business as usual and something they will build into the companies they run in 2010. Less change? Definitely not. More change? Highly likely.

4
The managers of the next millennium

> Remember when job hopping was considered bad?
> *Paul Kahn*, CEO SafeCard Services and former President of AT&T Universal Card

> Smith is not a born leader yet.
> *Anonymous*

> No one wants to follow a weak leader. He is the worst kind. You cannot rely upon his judgement because you don't know what he will do in a difficult situation. Much more respect and loyalty is given to the tough leader, the one who is not afraid to make difficult and even unpopular decisions, just as long as he is perceived to be decent and fair and reliable in his dealings with his subordinates.
> *Harold Geneen, Managing*, 1984

We know that the organization is changing, like a piece of plasticine it is being kneaded and shaped by unseen hands. We cannot stop that happening, but we all have the opportunity to get involved in the shaping of our own job, our own company, our own industry.

But, as was made clear in the previous chapter, the man or woman who might be the tough, hard-nosed cutter of people, assets and inventory may very well not be the person to lead the organization into the next phase: securing the ship and building for the future.

So what sort of leaders are we going to need and going to expect to take us to 2010? What attributes will they have to manifest to keep the ship sailing around the storms, without mutinies, without running aground? Remember, corporate success will increasingly be based on an ability to attract people to work in it – or for it – based on reputation as a place where the latest knowledge and skills are available. Tomorrow's leaders will have to remember that this is a key part of the 'compensation' package of the future.

A ground-breaking study – involving over 600 managers – by Management Centre Europe 'Business Leadership, what it takes today, what it means tomorrow' investigated what lower level executives thought of the abilities of their present leaders and particularly their chief executives.

As we prepare to enter a new millennium, the responses can provide real reasons to consider if, in our own organizations, the present top management are the ones equipped to do the job we are going to expect of them.

Management Centre Europe's study asked what business leaders do and what they should do. Reporting back, the 600-plus managers had this to say:

- Business leaders should be able to build effective teams (said 89 percent), but few (43 percent) thought their CEO could.
- Business leaders should know how to listen (said 84 percent), but less than half (47 percent) said their CEO did.
- CEOs should surround themselves with the right people (83 percent), but not many (42 percent) did.
- Only a quarter of the respondents (25 percent) said that a business leader should be motivated by power. But more than half (52 percent) said that was what got their CEO fired up.
- A minority (8 percent) put ruthless on their list of leadership attributes, but almost a quarter (23 percent) accused their top executive of being just that.
- Nearly all (98 percent) said that the main motivator for a business leader was money, power, ambition or a combination of all three. Just 2 percent said it had to do with personal satisfaction or self-realization.

In fact as the research showed, the only success criteria that today's leaders seem to have is the ability to make decisions on their own. As the study commented at the time, 'Added to the fact that their own people think they are energetic, strong-willed and ambitious, you are forced to come up with the picture of a lonely, autocratic, tough minded CEO.'

The survey also indicated that there could very well be a shortage of the right type of business leaders to meet future needs, and this is something that continues to be the great collective moan of top management – they cannot find the right people.

Another Management Centre Europe survey, 'What Managing Really Means', commented, 'the big concern is still a shortage of good executive talent. This issue is set to become the *bête noire* of organizations unless it is tackled head-on – and soon. Without the right people in place at the right time, too many executives will spend too much time trying to entice managers from other companies at the expense of what they should be doing: giving the customers what they want and ensuring long-term profit for the shareholders.'

But, although we are no longer looking for Rambo-style managers – but people to nurture and grow the organization, the market conditions of 2010 will still require managers with some pretty tough attributes. So, if research to date suggests that many top managers don't have what it will take, what are the attributes we should be looking for?

In a research project called 'The Manager of the Year 2000', Swiss-based executive search firm TASA asked a cross-section of managers to list and rate the qualities they thought the successful manager, running an enterprise in the next millennium, would need. In meeting the needs of the changing organization, it probably covers every eventuality. Perhaps no single manager has all these attributes, but the companies that survive will be those with top managements that embody many of these requirements, or have already seriously thought through their shortcomings and have definite plans in place to get the others.

Take a few moments, score these criteria and see just how many you or your collective top management meet. The result may make interesting reading (they are ranked by relative importance according to the research responses).

	Yes	No
1. A visionary, who can build and motivate a team to execute his vision, with strategic rather than tactical ability.		
2. Able to see the game changing and take effective action in a global context.		
3. Balance a respect of people with a sense of decision.		

	Yes	No
4. Broad experience and talent not taught in the classroom.		
5. Understands the corporate interface with outside constituencies – including the need for service, service, service.		
6. A creative individual who can bring the parts of an organization together to build something lasting, while able to provide stimulants for motivation, other than pay and promotion.		
7. Allows people to fail, but has the courage to face militant opponents.		
8. A highly informed, technically competent opportunist.		
9. Able to take something that works and turn it into a system.		
10. One hundred percent open-minded.		
11. Has infinite patience to listen, to tell, to help.		
12. Takes the decision today that is right in five years' time.		
13. Knows that historical data will be irrelevant.		

It is pretty safe to say that if you or your top managers don't have two-thirds of the above criteria – and are not prepared to work long and hard at getting the others – then the organization you work for is in trouble. Somewhere down the road to 2010 it is going to discover the future – the future it has created for itself by its own inaction – and the realization of what it's like won't be pleasant.

Richard Pascale gave some specific comments on the type of person he sees heading the management ranks of tomorrow. 'Is a Jack Welch [of General Electric], or anyone else who runs a large and complex system going to be any different fifteen years from now. I think that those kinds of executives who are first class today are pretty much the model for being a first-class executive fifteen years from now.

'I mean they are committed to growth and their own personal learning, they are just as much a facilitator as they are a decision-maker and they are very adept at social engineering.

>  The search for the new-style manager of 2010 must begin *now* amongst the middle management cadre.

I think there are people who have quite a bit of competence today, who in pretty much that form could be damn competent fifteen years from now.

The new-style manager

Pascale suggests that in the future, much of top management's role will change anyway – and, yes, we will see a new manager type emerge. His argument is that the real search for competent management for the future must begin now amongst the middle layers.

He thinks that there is an argument for the premise that people at the top by 2010 might be 'stewards of a system, where the real intelligence and initiatives come from self-organized teams'.

By the year 2010 he thinks that leadership will have to be 'exercised in a different way, in a less traditional way than command and control, but that leadership has to be more inspired and wiser.' But he adds, 'I'm not sure if that is a trend we are going to see occur, but it could.'

But he does see that the already redundant organizational Rambo – of the cut, cut, cut cult – is not the person to lead the next generation enterprise. 'The real difference isn't at the top. The real difference is in the middle level, the upper middle levels of management, where the selection process for what you are seeking as a manager for tomorrow is moving from the charismatic, decisive sort of Schwarzkopf type, to a person who is more of a facilitator and a listener; adept at designing processes that involve and enrol people.

'So those qualities in the early and middle level selection process will be more pronounced. At the end of the day, the people who run big companies – well at least some of the better ones – have the qualities we're talking about already.'

What all these people will have in common will be the ability to illustrate and articulate the new shared corporate values of the organization.

Bye, bye, Euromanager

The new management agenda that we all have to deal with will also provide an opportunity to bury one of the great European business myths – the Euromanager.

Once touted as the way things would have to be, this non-existent creature – who had a half-life in recruitment advertisements and headhunter's profiles – was supposed to be a man or woman, with an MBA, gifted in four or more languages and sensitive to cross cultural undercurrents as much as the balance sheet. He or she is popularly depicted as a German, who went to business school in France and is working for a British company in Italy.

Richard Hill, a Brussels-based business commentator, self-styled Euro-anthropologist and author of *We Europeans*, suggests that Euromanagers don't exist for two reasons. First, business is a global enterprise not a regional one. Second, despite fifty years of peace and the Single Market, Europe's businesses are still run on nationalistic lines.

Hill comments, 'In most companies, "Euromanager" is a catch phrase that has been almost prostituted and certainly used far too loosely. A lot of companies seem to have got a lot of attention for appearing to tackle Euro issues head on, but most of the time there's not really much happening under the surface.'

In a statement calculated to give Brussels' Eurocrats apoplexy, Hill suggests that, 'the only place that Euromanagers have ever flourished was in the subsidiaries of US corporations.'

Explaining that after the 1974 energy crisis, US corporations began a 'Europeanization' of their businesses in the Old World, Hill says that, 'they took their local nationals back and put Europeans in their place. They weren't worried about whether they were English, French or Spanish as long as they could do the job.'

And that, according to Hill at least, is why Euromanagers just do not flourish in Europe's corporations. 'In every country companies are dominated by a single culture, they are totally ethnocentric. European companies only do one of two things. They either send one of their own (German company sends a German to Milan) or they appoint a local national, but only after much soul searching.'

continued

> And, by way of example, he points to Asea Brown Boveri – a company that is being held up as *the* example of how Europe can revitalize its bruised and battered industries. 'Even they are really only Swedish and Swiss underneath, that's where the culture comes from.'
>
> The Americans, notes Hill, are just not like that. 'First and foremost the management style is different and that takes care of the cross-cultural pulls and pushes we have in Europe. Working for an American company in Europe, everyone becomes an American, that is the culture. It may be alien, but it is acceptable to many French, Dutch, Germans and Italians, though admittedly a lot just can't ever get used to that foreign culture in their own backyard and leave.'
>
> So, as we all learn to operate with a global mind-set, as we become valuable for our inherent skills, the Euromanager finally gets put to rest once and for all.

Autocrat or democrat?

Professor of Management at INSEAD, Jean-Claude Larréché, says, 'If one considers the management style for the leadership of the organization, I believe we are going toward a "benevolent dictator" or a "courageous preacher" as the winning style. This is a combination, in both cases, of two opposite dimensions. First the courage to make clear choices and, second the soft touch required to motivate the mass of people in an organization. The choice between one of the two expressions depends on which of the two is the most dominant.'

A wry comment from the usually irreverent consultant and international lecturer, Mike Kami who contrarily says 'All I really want is a top executive who is ten percent less stupid than another. It's not how great, but how less stupid!'

Perhaps the man or woman who will be best able to navigate through the thicket of tomorrow's complexities is the 'executive actor', a Jekyll and Hyde person, who – with neither of Larréché's personalities dominant – is able to change to meet present needs. Labeed Hamid, President of the Middle East Management Centre, suggests, 'Management styles will remain

– as they have for hundreds of years – dependent on the demands and pressures of that particular moment or situation. Autocratic management will always solve difficult problems or crises that demand a speedy solution, while democratic styles will remain a function of stable and steadily growing organizations. The best style for the year 2010 is the ability of an executive to switch from one style to another depending on the requirements of the situation and furthermore his ability to move his team behind him whenever the change takes place.'

Look now for the man or woman who produces and encourages consistency, *but* knows how to make mid-course corrections without losing credibility and support.

That idea gets strong support from consultant and author T.W. Kang in Tokyo. 'In terms of decision-making, the future manager will have to be very democratic in the information and analysis stage, using techniques like brain-storming. But once the decision is made, he or she will have to exert strong leadership in the execution phase. The difficulty is that given a rapidly changing environment, this leadership cannot lead to rigidity. This balance between consistency and necessary mid-course correction is going to be an art.'

He adds that the executive of 2010 will need to be 'multi-modal in one's cross-cultural abilities: maintaining one's identity and at the same time being able to behave outside the context of one's own upbringing.'

The glue of shared values

Consultant and author, John Humble, comments, 'As organizations becoming flatter and networked in style – as the boundary-less concept becomes reality – so shared values will be the glue which holds the human organization and its culture together. With the demise of command and control, old-fashioned bureaucracies cease to be important. Therefore, it follows that people will be better informed: sharing – rather than using information as a power tool – will be the norm.

Empowerment will not be an option, but a necessity in this world of rapid change, decentralization and flexibility.'

But Humble issues a warning that we should all take special heed of, 'companies will have to understand better that empowerment is a tough process. For example the careful selection and continuous training of people is the foundation for empowerment.'

And Humble quotes Richard Teerlink, the highly respected CEO of revitalized and renewed motorbike producer Harley-Davidson, on the need for constant training and the upgrade of skills 'If you empower dummies you get bad decisions faster.'

As the levels flatten and people are really capable of making their own decisions – armed, electronically with the tools to do it, the manager (the middle manager) finally slips into oblivion.

David Wimpress, Executive Chairman of Peritas the consulting arm of computer maker ICL, notes that Humble's point of training is a major issue. 'A lack of attention in this area has contributed to vast numbers of people being laid-off in many cases because organizations paid scant regard to the need to invest in training and development which anticipated changes in skills and competency requirements.'

'We have a great opportunity in Europe to liberate the potential of our people by providing career opportunity arising from programmes of delayering and devolution. Organizational change has flattened structures and we now have to create "hair-pin" career paths to replace the vertical.'

Learning to be executives

Learning to take those hair-pin curves and learning to enjoy the trip, comments Peter Drucker, is why managers will have to learn not to be managers. 'Managers from now on will be increasingly ineffectual. They have to learn to be executives. A manager by definition deals with subordinates. But even if people occupying a management position ten or fifteen years from now have people reporting to them they will not be subordinates. They will be knowledge workers who – if they are any good – know more than their supposed "boss". But increasingly also, the people with whom the executive will have to deal will be the people over whom he has no authority whatever: executives in joint-ventures, in partnerships, people in other companies, people employed by companies to whom major tasks have been outsourced.

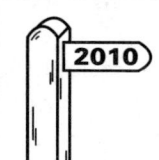
In the new working relationship we don't start with the question 'what do I want?' We start with the question, 'what do *they* want?'

'In many cases these people will work together with tomorrow's executives for many years, but they will not be subordinates, they will not be associates – they will be partners. To work with people like this requires a totally different mental attitude. Instead of starting out with the question, "what do I want?", one has to start with the question, "what do they want?" '

If you sit back for a moment and think about it there are lots of cases where this relationship between you, your organization and other service providers already exists and probably has for a long time; catering, legal services, transport, advertising – all of these and more are outsourced almost as a matter of course. It's just no one called it outsourcing before. So while the management commentators talk about deep change, much of it is, in fact, quite familiar to us.

In fitting all this together, Peter Drucker says that 'there is no one organizational structure that will be successful tomorrow. Companies and executives will have to learn that organizational structures are tools, and tools have to fit the job. We will continue to need hierarchy for the simple reason that someone in the organization has to have the final decision, or the organization degenerates into a permanent bull session.'

How much hierarchy is open to question and may well come down to the type of business you are in. All the same, with the exchange of ideas and knowledge as an important factor in improving both innovation and speed, flatter structures are going to encourage more sharing.

But we cannot entirely do without administration – no matter what the change doctors say. Despite what others might suggest, Drucker believes that we will 'have to have a considerable amount of bureaucracy, because without rules there is

English only

In all the interviews and research that went into preparing this book, one area that didn't get a lot of attention was the question of languages. Most management commentators stick to the old line, usually as an afterthought, that we need culturally aware managers who understand the needs of differing markets who will 'have multi-language skills'.

Interestingly enough, this doesn't appear to be the way it is going in reality. What is really happening is that everybody is learning to speak English. Whether this continued and outdated emphasis on speaking other languages can be explained by the fact that nearly all the people who insist that languages will be an important skill speak English – and are in most cases American – is not clear.

What is clear though, is that – despite what the French government think, with their new laws to ban English – the language of technology, the language of communications *is* English, with a very strong leaning towards American.

Think about it like this: no one with any sense in Brussels or Paris, or Dusseldorf is going to buy a computer system from a supplier or a technician who doesn't speak English. Reason? By the time the software manual is out in French, or German or Spanish, they are two generations out of date.

The French government is like a crazy King Canute trying to hold back the tide. What do they think kids watch in Marseille? Kids in Marseille watch MTV and swop pirate copies of English language software that their *ami* brought in from Los Angeles after a trip with his *mère* and *père* to Disneyworld.

How do you do business by fax, phone or E-mail with Khajakistan? You use English. The other alternative is to either have specialists who just happen to be good at their job and speak one of the hundreds of dialects – which is highly unlikely in your downsized, delayered, lean and mean organization – or you spend your time learning all of them yourself. This is about as useful as learning Latin because you are being posted to Latin America.

English dominates. It will always be helpful to speak other languages, but as the world – the business world at least becomes global – English takes over the communications systems of everyone.

only a mob. And yet we will have considerable extra ability to change and to create organizations that are focused on the task.'

Multi-tasking abilities

One of Europe's leading outplacement consultants, Win Nystrom sees the executives of tomorrow as people who – because of their requirement to be simultaneously a member of several different teams – 'will need multi-tasking abilities to serve the competing demands on their time and expertise. As owners of the process, both coaching and risk taking will be second nature to them.'

Suggesting a sort of high-tech, supercharged executive, Nystrom goes on to describe his vision of the manager of tomorrow as 'a glutton for change and a speed demon. His or her expectations of others will be dwarfed by the discipline they exert on themselves. Technologically at the cutting edge of their fields they will constantly augment their broad quiver of competencies.'

Agreeing with Drucker's view of tomorrow, Nystrom expects that 'Management styles as such will be less relevant than the ease of assuming simultaneous roles. In the absence of organizational titles and hierarchies, project driven "roles" perpetually shift with current and anticipated customer needs.'

Re-skill as many employees as you can, but also hire in people with new skills. New blood is vital to an organization's future.

Re-engineering's *eminence grise*, Jim Champy, has a very clear view – that supports Nystrom's multi-functional executive – on where all these pressures of organizational change are leading. 'As the work changes, you must re-skill your people and hire others for skills you can't get from retraining. This requires us to adopt a new covenant with employees. In a re-engineered organization it's no longer feasible to guarantee a job for life or a job for good performance. The skills we now need are changing dramatically. Management's obligation to workers is to help them develop the skills they'll need to be successful in or outside the organization. I call this adding to a worker's portfolio of marketable assets.'

To that end, all of us have to sit down and assess just where we – as individuals – are today and where we would like to be – or think we need to be – in five, ten or fifteen years time. It might look like a long way away, but planning for change, and knowing how to get skills you don't even know today that you'll need tomorrow is part of your success script for 2010.

Champy takes the process of what the manager will look like a stage further, by talking about how tomorrow's organization will need Humble's cultural glue to function. 'First, to ensure that the company's culture doesn't block re-engineering we must ask what kind of culture we have and what kind we need for the new business process to operate. Culture in a re-engineered organization becomes critical for another reason. It replaces structure and rules of governance as the mechanisms for guiding people's behaviour. With more work becoming self-managed and fewer managers to check and recheck the work, you need something other than management structure and rules to guide workers.'

As in the last chapter, Champy continues to stress – to warn – that 'you're not done with re-engineering after you've done it once. You have to constantly ask these questions about purpose, process, people, culture. These become the defining questions for management. While they aren't entirely new questions for managers, they carry a much higher importance than ever before.'

Self-managed, self career-directed

Of course, with all this change and upheaval going on, organizations are bound to throw up some mavericks. Just as a salesperson today is totally different from someone working in accounts payable or human resources, so executives in 2010 will be diversified, and non more so in how they adapt.

While some may not adapt at all and will drift to other professions, the strong survivors will make the new environment their own, growing professionally and being totally at ease in this new world. Their very adaptability will be their passport to success. The old idea of praising employees who were 'steady' workers will be an anathema.

Outplacement consultant Win Nystrom sees a 2010 with the new-style executives 'working in a collection of activity modules that may dissolve or be rerouted to another project even before the final product or service reaches a particular client. Core groups of friends/alliances/partners with a shared mission and committed to shared client service values will dominate.'

It is almost as if every department and sub-department of a major organization had been individually privatized. In a way, little has really changed. Perhaps the notional security of the corporation has disappeared, but in its place is another security – that of knowing a good job deserves its reward and will continue to do so.

Nystrom adds to his check-list for the specialist survivor of 2010. 'Self-managed, self-motivated, self-career directed, these versatile professionals will drive multiple missions through to completion, moving from project to project, heedless of company boundaries.'

Exploring the darker side

Richard Pascale shares this view of a possible work world that will operate much differently from today. 'The dark side to this is that you could end up with an industrial peasantry where you effectively have a pre-industrial revolution sort of fragmented and isolated group of individuals, who kind of come in and provide part-time services when there is a need and then basically disappear out of the system: without a community, without a sense of identity, without access to things like pensions and medical coverage and the other things that large organizations historically have provided.'

Philippe Alloing, European Director Human Resources for consulting firm A.D. Little, in Paris, warns that there is a real risk of companies 'selecting lonely wolves, hopping from one place on earth to another with no root or attachment anywhere'.

But Alloing holds out some hope that not every manager of today is just going to become a multi-tasking super executive. 'What I witness though is that the vast majority of would-be managers in Europe (it's different in the USA and Asia) are looking for balance between private and professional interests and within the professional sphere between responsibilities and socialization.'

The rewards

Alloing's view, not shared by everyone, is that 'High gross income will become less of a motivator than opportunities to pursue personal interests alongside professional development.' This Alloing says will be achieved 'through flexibility of assignments, acceptance of family needs and benefits suited to actual needs, changing with age.'

 **2010** Expect pay plans to be turned upside-down. Like sports stars, top performers will have short, highly charged careers, with big rewards for the top goal scorers.

But with no jobs for life, and no guarantees of repeat business even if your work was good, executives are going to expect and demand high compensation. Like soccer players or basketball players whose earning periods are limited by their age and stamina, it will be important for the specialists and executives of tomorrow to score, a lot and often, in their peak years.

Those who are still on board will need to be given a piece of the action, profit shares or company stock to ensure their commitment and high performance. As Mike Kami says, 'retain people by a fraction of the action!' and he also says that, 'performance-related pay – with no ceiling' should be the norm.

'Engineers should get ten percent of the action for a patent, sales people should make more than their CEO.' He mentions as an example what happened to one super salesman we have all heard of – Ross Perot at IBM. They had a cap – a ceiling – on compensation. On January 28th he hit the cap. They wouldn't give him any more money so he left.'

Kami also points out that one of the failings of many companies is that they don't know how to 'recognize and tolerate talent!' That he says is something we must all do, 'even if it dresses different, smells different, works nights ... and especially if it's the type of person that the HR directors of large corporations won't like!'

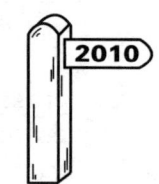

If you destroy the old control structure there has to be something else to take its place ... and that's creating a system that lets the employees control themselves: tricky to do, nice when it works.

Tom Bonoma also thinks that pay and other forms of reward are important and they should reflect what people contribute and not be structured. 'Everyone should share in the profits and if a salesman doesn't make more money than I do then I am upset. Don't ever cap their abilities.' But he also notes that the necessary destruction of old stereotypes and systems should apply through the whole organization even to letting the newly empowered 'put anything on their business card so long as it helps them sell'.

Bonoma, wisely realizes that this new-age corporation, with a reduced headcount and possibly less business areas is going to be lean and mean, but it is going to need some serious love and attention to build new alliances, create a new glue between employer and employees.

'You've got to get the hunger back,' he advises, 'and the only way to do that is give total empowerment backed up by example. If they stay and work all night – you stay as well. Children and people will do no more than they see someone else doing. If the top guy leaves at four, so do they.'

Talking to managers on the front line it seems that pay – reward – is a real issue. And in Europe – where countries like Belgium institute two-year salary freezes that make a joke of performance-related pay schemes – we will see that, unless governments begin to do more to motivate managers by reviewing personal tax structures, there won't be any managers left to manage the brave new corporations of 2010. They will all be investment bankers in Bermuda instead.

The conclusion is simple. There are no jobs for life anymore. Everyone will have to manage their own careers. As a senior executive of IBM – the company that just a few short years ago prided itself on full employment – said at a recent European human resources conference 'We are in an age of high competition and high uncertainty. We maintained a policy of full employment until very recently and believed that it was good. Now we know that, in the new environment, affordability becomes the rule and employees must stand and share with us these new realities.' Hundreds of thousands of managers around the world believed that if you had your corporate niche – including your annual increase – your job was better than money in the bank. But the new realities could spawn a harder and less productive attitude.

Unless it is managed well, the danger is that a 'get it while you can' attitude will prevail. It is going to take some very able managers to make the organizations of tomorrow work and make the people who should be tomorrow's executives want to come and work in them.

The manager in society

Richard Pascale makes an interesting point that, perhaps, few of us have considered, but as we, or if we continue to, pursue our management careers perhaps we should. 'I think that unbidden and somewhat unexpected many people who chose management as a career have found themselves collectively – not individually – thrust into a role in society that they didn't bargain for. I mean most people who went in for management did not at the time see it as a particularly high status calling, as compared to say a doctor. As it turns out, the well-being of our nations is more influenced by our GNP and our balance of payments and a few other things, than by our nuclear arsenal and our sciences. So people who are managers – by virtue of being stewards of those organizations that determine a nation's standing on the globe – are, I think, going to be subjected to increased attention, because they are important players and stakeholders in our society. I think this is as current today and I think it will be so in the next fifteen years.'

This thought that the manager, the business executive, is a key cog in the way the world turns obviously puts a great responsibility on the shoulders of business leaders. But it also raises other issues. The re-engineering processes, the massive amount of change that has coloured the work life of many of us is something that we are just getting around to. Moreover, many business people, not to mention others outside business, in the professions, in academia, in government, don't fully realize what a profound revolution is going on. There are thousands of businesses which are not undergoing change, at their peril perhaps, but they are still not doing anything to meet new challenges.

So if, as Richard Pascale suggests, there is a greater, societal, role this is a profound responsibility for the business executive. Therefore, shouldn't more be done to explain a great deal more about what is going on inside private enterprise. Isn't it, in some way imperative that people outside the business society understand what the mass lay-offs are all about. Perhaps there is a new business opportunity for some entrepreneur: explaining to the world and helping the world learn from the changes that market forces have brought – and are still bringing – to our corporations, large and small.

What to watch for

- The best people will go to firms that have a reputation for providing knowledge, skills and access to the latest technology. If your company cannot do that, all it will get are second-class people and you will become second-class as well. Management's obligation becomes clear. To help and encourage employees to develop skills they will need when they are no longer required. It's called employability.
- If you're running a company and want to see it grow, think along these same lines; invest in skills and most important the ability to give your people skills – without that the best – even the best of the rest – will pass you by.
- You must be committed to growth and personal learning and work in companies that subscribe and practise this.
- Companies must start looking for their new manager *now*. He or she is somewhere in the middle ranks, but needs to be recognized quickly to be an effective new age executive.
- Benevolent dictator or courageous preacher, the jury's out, but it really doesn't matter. The key word is respect;

the key ability, leadership; the key trait, toughness under fire.
- You will have to manage people you have no power over. As 'do it this way' drops from the business vocabulary, it will take new powers of persuasion to get things done. Managers who learn that early, will succeed faster.
- The winners will be executives and specialists who can do a multiplicity of tasks simultaneously. No one is going to care too much about your management style if you can get five things done at once.
- Capping compensation kills. Although pure performance-related pay may not be the answer, limiting earnings – or other forms of compensation – is a foolish policy that ultimately starves an organization of top performers.

5
The currency of knowledge

> We are about half-way through one of the great transformations of the world – a transformation in which centuries are compressed into decades. This transformation is from a society in which the financial and physical capital has been the dominant business resource to one in which the dominant resource will be knowledge.
>
> *Peter Drucker*

> You have learned something. That always feels at first as if you had lost something.
>
> *George Bernard Shaw*

In the new world of knowledge, where any organization's largest assets are located between the ears of its employees, the biggest challenge for 2010 will not be to know information, but to keep on knowing information. And that is going to take some doing. Reason? All the experts conclude that the knowledge we need to be effective in our jobs is going to change very rapidly – once every three years or so, is the current time-frame.

It is up to you to: stay ahead, stay smart, stay employable.

That need to keep learning has spawned business phrases like 'the learning organization', which has been held up as the example of the direction corporations should be moving towards. But, more and more, the onus will fall on the shoulders of the individual to stay ahead, stay smart, stay employable. The company provides the tools and the individual brings the knowledge to effectively employ and innovate with those tools.

What is clear, now is that it is becoming commonly acceptable to all that jobs for life are gone forever, is that the only responsibility that an employer has to the employees is to prepare them for tomorrow. Make them employable in the outside world when they are no longer needed in the company.

This of course will create new elite companies. The enterprises of tomorrow who really help their employees, keep them at the peak of performance through continuous learning, will be the places to work – because you will always get a job with another company eager for those skills you've picked up. Once again – perhaps in different skills and with a different approach – the best will train for the rest.

Make yourself marketable

To put into context the ongoing learning curve we will need to be employable in the next fifteen years, here's a sobering thought from consultant and author John Humble. 'If there aren't going to be cradle-to-grave jobs anymore, the secret of success will be employability. You don't own a job, but you are marketable to a wide range of people. To do that you will need to keep learning as a constant process.'

And to illustrate just how far we have come in a few decades, Humble provides some sobering food for thought. 'My father probably got through his working life by doubling his knowledge, for me it has possibly been a factor of fifty times. For the next generation, who knows what it will take to stay ahead.'

A great deal more, not just to qualify and get that degree or that diploma but to stay employed.

Maverick management commentator Mike Kami knows, 'If you are not 100 times smarter than you were five years ago – you don't count.'

And in case there is any doubt that knowledge – allied to an ability to update and adapt that knowledge – is going to take control of our collective futures, here's an extract from the *Financial Times*, which stated in a report that the middle class in the USA is being divided by its levels of education and skills, according to Robert Reich, US Labor Secretary.

Reich said, 'The deepest divisions [in US society] aren't based on race or on national origin or on geography; they're based on the abilities of individuals to make their way in an increasingly turbulent society.' He said that the middle class had splintered into three groups: an 'underclass', isolated from the core economy and walled off from hope; an 'overclass', who profitably rode the changes in the economy; and the bulk of the population, an 'anxious' class ... pulled and stretched by the need to work two or more jobs to keep a family solvent ... by the spectre that today's job will disappear tomorrow. The answer to the growing divisions, he says, is education. Expanding skills, particularly in technology-related fields, in-house training programmes and keeping potential high-school drop-outs in education longer, all help to build a new middle class, he believes.

That's someone talking about society as a whole and how changing business conditions – particularly technology – are already impacting the lives of all of us. At the business level, at the executive level, I suspect – probably not as clearly defined yet – that there are both companies and individuals who fall into those three categories: an 'underclass', that still hasn't seen the need for change, and most particularly are not yet aware that knowledge is taking over as the prime asset; the 'overclass', who are already ahead of the game and are being recognized for their foresightedness as the organizations people are clamouring to work for; the 'anxious' class, still not quite sure which way to jump, knowing it's the eleventh hour and they still haven't finished their homework.

Certainly, we are not all perfect, and in this new race for knowledge most of us are just getting away from the starting gate. So, unless by some complete fluke we all got it right, education – the right sort – is going to be a bigger and bigger issue as we head toward 2010.

Education in disarray

But this emphasis on better education and more of it poses two questions. First, are the schools and colleges of today equipped to teach the right curriculum for future needs? Second, is business doing a great deal to explain to the educationists what its requirements are and will be? The answer to both of these seems to be – with a few exceptions – a resounding 'no'.

Even in Japan it seems that the much admired cooperation between business and education isn't completely solving business requirements.

There's not much use teaching marketing to students who don't want to go out and sell.

Consultant and author, T.W. Kang reports, 'What educational institutions need to do is to get away from any residuals of "ivory-tower" mentality and get very close to the front line of the business. Current schools are at their weakest when it comes to teaching selling, manufacturing and cross-cultural problem solving. Think how many business school students cannot sell one pencil to anyone out there on the street.

'Schools should create team-building exercises where students are asked to structure a simple manufacturing line from scratch and analyse the work-flow by actually manufacturing a product.

'In terms of cross-cultural communication and problem solving, students from different countries should be required to engage in role-playing exercises which are set up for constructive cross-cultural confrontation, which they must resolve. Having this experience in school, where there are no financial and political pressures, is a unique experience which students will never have a chance to encounter once they enter the real world.'

Further views on how to educate the leaders of tomorrow come from a Management Centre Europe research study that looked at the best ways to make sure that the organization got the well-rounded, forward thinking top executive it needed? The poll, 'Business Leadership – what it takes today, what it means tomorrow', showed that a mixture of experience and education is essential. In the opinions of more than 600 European managers, the best ways to develop a business leader are:

- On-the-job experience with a good role model as a superior   68 percent

- Education and experience in a
  multi-country environment   66 percent
- Exposure to more than just one business   65 percent
- Building on the basis of an initial business
  school education   31 percent
- Exposure to areas other than business   20 percent
- Getting thrown into the business 'at the
  deep end' and told to 'sink or swim'   11 percent

The fact that there are still organizational Rambos about – the 11 percent who think people can survive unnurtured – might be disturbing, but what is most disturbing about this MCE poll is that less than one-third of the respondents thought an initial business school education counted for all that much.

Out in the real world that T.W. Kang talks about, there is a lot of dissention – even amongst academics – that schools and colleges and particularly business schools are going to have to make sweeping changes if they are to have anything to offer to industry.

The bricks and mortar factory

Former senior member of the Wharton School's faculty, Richard Pascale says, 'I think the business schools are – to overstate it – dinosaurs. They are tied to a bricks and mortar factory that forces them to try to utilize that plant and equipment and therefore drag participants to their facilities rather than go and use the facilities in the organization.'

Forecasting much trouble, as organizations demand better service and more relevant products from the academic establishment, he says, 'They tend to work on the basis of serving heterogeneous audiences rather than single company audiences. And they have problems with the faculty – and the interest of the faculty – that make it a somewhat hit or miss proposition that a company is going to be well served by the sort of standard "plain vanilla" offering of business school.'

Liam Fahey, who teaches at both Babson College in the USA and Cranfield School of Management in the UK concurs, 'The situation is probably worse in the USA than in Europe and right now business schools in the USA have some intense soul-searching to do. A lot of their paradigms are clearly outmoded.

Learning isn't always formal

Learning doesn't just come from formal systems, it is something that employees can develop for themselves. It goes on in every organization where the employees find the 'right' way to do it never mind what management really think is going on. A useful illustration of the informal learning process was given by John Seely Brown, Xerox's Chief Scientist, at a recent top management forum. He said, 'The real challenge is we have to get a new set of glasses to see in our existing organizations what is really happening. To go – in this knowledge economy – from producing volume to producing value.'

Insisting that 'techno-macho solutions are not the only way', Seely Brown gave the example of sending social anthropologists to travel with Xerox sales people to find out what really happened when they were at work.

He said that when Xerox had unthinkingly broken up the sales system – giving them few opportunities to meet, they recreated it informally. 'We in management thought that the time telling stories was a waste of time,' he said, 'so we pulled out the most important place where learning was really going on.'

Xerox's decision prompted drastic action by the representatives and technical support staff. They 'created a radio system so they could speak to each other' when they had problems in the field. 'This was the real expert system,' said Seely Brown, who emphasized that we must face that there are two work systems, 'one that talks about the structuring of work and one that talks about how that work gets done.'

Also, a lot of their faculty is clearly not committed to learning in the sense of updating themselves and they're still teaching the tools and techniques they were teaching five, ten even fifteen years ago. Moreover, many of the teachers despise practical experience, because they don't have it themselves.'

Paul Kahn, now the CEO at SafeCard Services and former head of AT&T World Card, comments that 'my sense is that colleges are behind trend lines, they don't keep up, but neither do managers.' All the same he points out that there are key issues for corporations 'like quality, customer service and the focus on people that are either underemphasized or not on the curriculum.'

Kahn, who admits that in his own college days so much of what he learned he never used, thinks that there has to be a massive injection of equipment and leadership into colleges to ready them for tomorrow's needs. Also, he says that the focus on the analytical 'teaches you the mechanics but not the leadership and inspiration you need.'

And it is that inspirational aspect that the chief executive of tomorrow and his top management team are really going to have to work on and get right to make any kind of success of the enterprise of the next century.

Kahn adds, 'if I was doing it over,' he suggests, 'I would use college as a broad base, not as a specialization.' While he feels that business is not doing enough to dictate what they need to have in the manager for the future, he and many others realize that there is fundamental weakness in the inherent costs of changing the system to something that would work effectively. Certainly in talks with academics and other commentators, the grim truth is that education is falling further behind today's needs, both in the ability to provide the right curriculum and in their inability – largely because of the investment required – to upgrade technologically.

 Don't be a specialist, learn to think as broad as possible.

The need to 'de-specialize' is taken up by Jim Champy as yet another re-engineering challenge. 'Business schools, like business itself, are fragmented into narrow specialities. Today's curricula will have to recognize the fact that the work of managers and the work of workers is changing dramatically. Specialities, such as marketing, finance and organizational change, can no longer be taught as narrow subjects.'

Champy goes on to describe his ideals for teaching business in the world of tomorrow. 'I believe the model curriculum will look like re-engineered work and re-engineered management processes: courses on understanding deeper, fundamental changes in markets and industries; mobilizing the organization and enabling it to make big changes fast; the management of work teams; processes such as customer acquisition, concept to market and customer service. Narrowly focused courses will still be around, but they will be specialist courses.'

But, like other commentators, Champy sees all this as a tough to make it work switch-over in mind-set for those involved. 'This won't be an easy transition for many schools. Their tenure structure reinforces the fragmentation of their departments more rigidly than a lot of companies. If you are a tenured professor of marketing, that's your life. You don't move around very easily. And you don't change your long-held ideas – for which you are regarded as an expert – very easily. So this sense of entitlement to position and speciality makes it difficult to change the curricula of academic institutions.'

The arm-lock on education that currently exists is going to provide a crisis not to far down the road to 2010, particularly when we take into account the widely-held view that tomorrow's executive needs a broader, not a narrower education. As academics hold on to their programmes – almost all deeply entrenched in specializations of one kind or another, so their courses will be seen as increasingly irrelevant by the executives of tomorrow and those who seek to employ them.

MBA blues?

After practically seventy years of academic and consulting life, Peter Drucker's view that the day of the MBA degree – straight after college – is probably over deserves a lot more than passing attention. What does Drucker see of the relationship between academia and business as we head to the next century?

'Our colleges and universities and business schools need to realize that the traditional MBA no longer serves much of a purpose – it is a waste of young people and makes sense only after they have had five or six years' experience. Then it becomes very meaningful indeed.'

As a senior academic at a school that has a reputation for being both successful and up-to-date, Jean-Claude Larréché of INSEAD, the best-known business school in Europe, makes the point that, 'the number one responsibility of any school is admissions. It is at this level that one selects the leaders of tomorrow. This is the great value that recruiters buy when they come to recruit at any campus.'

And Larréché makes the practical point that, 'given the challenges of the future and the requirements placed on the management style of the twenty-first century executive, admission requirements should go way further than just number-crunching capabilities.'

Anything else? 'Yes, beyond admissions, the most important requirement is for the curriculum to change from a knowledge orientation to an emphasis on action and communication.'

One of the predicted fall-outs of academia's failure to meet what business feels will be its upcoming requirements, has been the rise of the do-it-yourself movement. As Northwestern University's Philip Kotler observes, 'We do need to assure ourselves that training facilities are adequate to deal with the new challenges. While we will always need programmes that prepare people for business, book learning goes only so far. We need much more emphasis on business experience itself, particularly in global marketing.'

 Corporate universities are just coming into vogue, they have the facilities, the equipment, the courses and the resources that business needs: expect more of them.

'That's why corporations are putting together their own universities: the Motorola University, the Hamburger University and so on.' So the forecast from Kotler and others is that as businesses seek people with more knowledge, but want people who can be constantly useful and know the 'way of the firm', so the concept of the 'corporate university' is set to expand. As knowledge becomes ever more important as a tradeable currency for tomorrow, growing your own talent makes a lot of sense.

That sort of diversification would please MORI's Nick Winkfield who pleads for academics to, 'stop using the same course designs, so that we can end up with a variety of skills, attitudes and styles'. As he explains, 'if all managers learn from the same teachers, they will all make the same decisions and the games will all end in a stalemate.'

> **Technology will change teaching**
>
> One of the reasons that traditional colleges and business schools are finding it difficult to keep up is the huge investment it will take to update learning. Basically, learning in college hasn't changed much in fifty years and the main technology is still a piece of chalk and a blackboard.
>
> But as Lester Thurow, former Dean of the Sloan School of Management at MIT points out, 'the electronic revolution will dramatically change teaching'. If the school can afford to invest.
>
> Not only that. As the debate continues on whether business schools have a future, the IT age is already posing a challenge for them. As Thurow says, 'Why go to a third rate school, when I will be able to stay at home and watch the equivalent of an Einstein on an interactive electronic system?'
>
> Thurow, who has already taught on interactive video from Boston to Singapore, 'where you control the camera so you can see who's paying attention,' sees this as a real revolution for the future. The elitism of top schools is changed as everyone can, theoretically at least, enrol and have access.
>
> Labeed Hamid, of the Middle East Management Centre agrees with Thurow, and adds that 'surely an international training TV cable network is not too difficult to imagine. Certainly, with the need for new knowledge, a service of this kind on a global scale must be developed soon.'
>
> 'Technology will change the way people learn, with the ability to examine interactive cases,' says George Day of the Wharton School. 'We will have access to people and ideas from everywhere.'

Corporate strategist John Elkins agrees with the growth of the corporate education system, but adds to Kotler's comments like this, 'The public education system failed in its basic tenet to provide for business needs. So now corporations themselves must absorb these educational needs – and fund them in some cases. I think the real question now is whether public education can survive without a revolution, but there is no doubt that the corporation will have to be more involved to offer the basics of education.'

But what business wants is not the basics of education. What business wants, and expects to get one way or another, is an effective way to keep high performing people, probably already in senior management, constantly up-to-date and able to recognize the opportunities of the future before anyone else. So how are they going to achieve that, with the moribund academic institutions they have today? The answer is they're not. Already they are abandoning the well trodden paths and 'going around the system', building their own programmes that meet the very specific needs of the key people in their company.

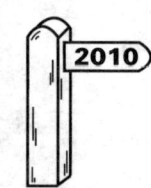

The smart business academics are already doing their own deals on consulting with corporations, cutting out the college middle-men. Look for this trend to increase and plan to use it to get a sharper focus on your new ideas.

Predicting that this is the way that much of tomorrow's education will go, Richard Pascale says, 'Increasingly, the sophisticated companies – which are more and more numerous – have a pretty good handle on the current body of ideas. I mean those ideas are well marketed today through a variety of means, videos, speeches by successful professors and so forth.

The active learning experience

'So what is it that is needed in a company beyond hearing a professor from Harvard lecture, or seeing him on video? What is really needed is an active learning experience, where your own team goes out and deals with a real problem, and you have that expert – that professor – involved with you on the scene. Or in some close to real-life situation where the learning, the ideas of new concepts is a third of what's going on. The other two-thirds is getting your team to internalize the ideas and use them powerfully against your competition. This takes the form of a sort of helping/enabling relationship rather than a classic teaching relationship.' What corporations are saying is, 'our needs have changed and we also need answers and ideas faster – let's cut out the middle man.' Just like they have delayered and cut the middle managers from their own organizations.

And how does this affect the business school, what does it all mean long-term for them if this does become the prevailing trend?

Pascale continues, 'now a business school – and the whole design of a business school as an institution – adds very little value to this process. At best it is a sort of extra broker or intermediary in a relationship that is more successfully handled by a faculty member dealing personally with a client. So if you look at the Harvards and Stanfords of this world, what is in fact occurring is that the institution called the business school is losing more and more of its historical control over the faculty. Because, neither the faculty nor the customer is well served by being imprisoned by the demands of the institution. So, effectively, there is a coalition being formed by the individual faculty members and the customers, to go outside the institution and do the deal or work that needs to be done.'

On the basis of Pascale's comments it may be too late for Drucker's suggestion that, 'The most meaningful experience and the greatest contribution, organized education can make to business, to organizations and to society is to continue the advance of already highly educated, successful, adult executives. Every business school in the world needs to reorganize itself, so that at its centre is a very demanding, long-term programme of continuing education for successful adults in organizations.'

It might be that the best and the brightest have already been there and are now well ahead of the game, doing what all the experts say is the right thing: innovating; leading from the very front; confounding the opposition. That this marks a break with tradition really doesn't matter as all the rest of tradition probably went with the change process anyway. So why not educate your people in the most pragmatic, cost-effective way possible.

 The real challenge is to get the college drop-out – the entrepreneur – back to school. Do that and you have yourself a super-manager.

Tom Bonoma agrees with that, but adds one important additional factor, the challenge of how to get to the real entrepreneur and teaching them the value of knowledge. 'I've rarely ever seen an entrepreneur in a business school, those who go to school are risk averse. The challenge is to get at those who are successful, but don't value the education model. That is a challenge for tomorrow, get those people and make them better; get the entrepreneurs and find out how to make them better.'

Getting that entrepreneur back to school could be a useful idea for many firms that are starved of real talent. As business requirements demand a broader base of experience and top managements begin to reject narrow-based talent, the entrepreneur, rounded out by the right business education input could be a major plus in any hard hustling organization of the future.

That's something on Bonoma's mind when he picks up on Drucker's point that an MBA can be useful *after* you've been on the battle lines for five or six years, Bonoma says, 'If I could stand in front of all the thousands of MBA students my first questions would be, "Why are you here? Why do you associate formal education with management ability?" '

Bonoma, like others feels that there are many 'industry specific and company specific experiences that you cannot find in a school. 'Listen,' he says, 'my colleague who teaches quality has never been in a factory like that. I would challenge whether business school isn't better done by example.'

Liam Fahey adds further fuel to the argument that business schools are not the way to go, 'If you think about the training executives will need, business schools don't even come close. For example they need to be much more cross-cultural than that.'

However Fahey doesn't just criticize the business schools and their like for this current state of affairs. 'The raw, naked truth is that most executives have little or no feel for the changes that are taking place and what they need to do to make themselves better.'

Tough words perhaps, but with more than a grain of truth. Few executives are in the vanguard of the changes that are sweeping through industry. Most in fact are sitting on the sidelines watching and worrying. Whether you blame the individuals for not being more aware or blame their companies for not helping them face up to change, the fact is that not enough is being done to really educate the majority of managers. Not only are there just a tiny minority who ever get to business school (and those numbers are even smaller in Europe), but few really get further effective management development.

But teachers like Liam Fahey, at least part of the time, live in eternal optimism.

Charging that, 'one of the ironies is that, as the technological revolution has speeded up our intellectual capacities to use it haven't got better, they've probably got worse.' Fahey suggests that 'forces will operate within organizations to make the new teaching requirements happen'.

No option but to educate

This isn't a story with a set of options. As business gets more complex, as it gets more out of the direct control of the top management through the creation of the empowered, flatter structures, so the continued education of those at the top, and the knowledge workers just a level or two below will become paramount.

As Mike Kami says, 'Education is knowledge, and we need to double it every four years or so. If you don't as an individual constantly seek knowledge and self-renew you will become a liability.

'And if you get a CEO who says, "hey, I don't need this!", it won't work that way, because those below won't respect the CEO anymore.'

Kami ends, 'And remember, we've got to teach the CEO to understand. Not to say "I've got six people to advise me." '

The final assumption is that the business school as we know it today having failed – thus far – to reinvent itself to meet the needs of tomorrow, will slip into a peripheral role as far as the corporations it has sought to serve are concerned.

Replacing it will be much more tailor-made education, that is purpose developed for individual corporations and will focus on their needs and their learning requirements.

It would seem that, just as the leading management academics and commentators are forecasting flatter organizations with fewer permanent staff and a cadre of mobile, flexible specialists to support it, they in their own profession are already treading the same path!

What is certain from all the discussion, advice and ideas is that tomorrow's world is a world where knowledge is our principal asset, where learning how to learn must be a paramount objective – not just once but as a continuous process – to be able to take on board the ideas of the future – not forgetting to discard the old ones along the way.

Most important for the knowledge worker of tomorrow is where they choose to work. Access to advanced learning, access to breakthrough technologies will be part of what the best employers offer. Making choices about learning, as much as about doing, will become yet another twenty-first century imperative.

Once again, it is those who make the right choices early who will reap the benefits. All the same, it seems that to write-off the business schools too quickly could be a major mistake. While there is no doubt that they will have to invest hugely in new equipment to make their teaching relevant, and will also have to change the way they teach, there is one thing that should keep them around well into the next millennium – past reputation.

The Harvards, MITs, Sloans, and INSEADs of this world won't vanish tomorrow. And at the end of the day, it will be interesting to see if Hamburger University, or Pizza College gain – despite their obvious usefulness – a reputation that can match the Ivy League schools, not to mention what a would-be high-flyer would rather have on his CV.

What to watch for

- In the new business world only *you* can make yourself marketable. So to stay employable the advice is *keep learning*.
- It is widely agreed that education – more specifically business education – has got it wrong. Failure to make massive upgrades in equipment, or throw out obsolete teaching methods will open the market to new entrants.
- Wealthier companies with eyes to the future are going it alone and building their own universities that teach what they want people to know.
- Companies that need new ideas and new thinking for their top management are doing one-on-one deals with

top business academics. A trend that could break cosy relationships for ever.
- Top performers, anxious to stay up-to-date, not to mention ahead, are demanding and getting active learning experiences that involve the teaching of top academics and real-life, real-time exercises.
- Specialist executive development organizations are making massive investments in new technology so the business world can plug-in on-line through their computer anytime, anywhere. All the same, face-to-face interaction is not going to disappear, just get better.

6

Cuddling up to the customer

> Customers are not supposed to present the great mystery!
>
> *Tom Bonoma*

> Business without marketing is like winking at a girl in the dark ... you know what you are doing, but no one else does.
>
> *Anonymous*

There have been a lot of battles on the way, but there can be little doubt that, overall, marketing has won the day as the pre-eminent discipline of the corporation of the next millennium. While there may still be room in some of those fat-cat corporations, that have not yet heeded the winds of change, for the brutal tactics of the cut, cut, cut executive who manages on the numbers alone, essentially it is a marketing organization that has emerged as the model for the modern management structure. So maybe you should check out your organization and see where the power – where the emphasis – lies.

What is being firmly touted these days is not just that marketing has won the battle of the departments, but that we all have to be marketers. This change is very significant, for what it suggests is that companies driven by other disciplines, or by senior management from other disciplines (finance, legal affairs, etc.) are going to have difficult battles ahead, if the top of the organization fails to become properly market oriented.

But it isn't really that marketing has won a decisive battle. What has happened is that marketing – or whatever we will now choose to call it – has become the all pervading mission of everyone in an organization. In other words marketing is now a label that covers all the functions. Indeed marketing becomes a cross-functional way of thinking about everyone's responsibility, everyone's job and everyone's focus. And as we head to the new millennium, this total emphasis on marketing, on the customer as the ultimate arbiter of a corporation's success, will become the norm.

So whether today you see your discipline, your profession, as manufacturing, human resources, logistics or finance, tomorrow – in the re-engineered firm, where the products and services you offer are part of a process – you will be a marketer.

Surprisingly, this isn't really a blinding truth that has suddenly come upon us, it has been evident for a very long time and some of the world's best corporations have been practising parts of the total process for many years, but now all the pieces are beginning to click together and we are seeing the emergence of the total marketing – totally customer focused – corporation.

Indeed, some trace the whole concept of marketing as the mind-set for the whole business back just over 40 years to a predecessor of General Electric's Jack Welch. Writing to shareholders, the then President, John McKitterick, described his vision as the, 'marketing concept that integrates marketing into each phase of the business. Thus marketing, through its studies and research, will establish for the engineer, the design and manufacturing person, what the customer wants in a given product, what price he, or she, is willing to pay and where and when it will be wanted.' Four decades later, in a very different business world, many companies are just beginning to heed his words.

True, the management thinkers with a focus on marketing, like Levitt and Kotler have been urging us in this direction for a long time, but it is only now, as technology – and specifically information technology – changes our organizations, that marketing finally becomes the total driver of the firm. Or rather that the focus changes totally, so that the customer, the clients, drive what we, the suppliers provide.

The corporate marketing mind-set

During a 1994 international marketing conference, marketing's pre-eminent spokesman, Philip Kotler buried the discipline as a stand alone department, saying 'there's no such thing as marketing – the marketing mind-set now covers the corporation.'

>  The whole *raison d'être* for your company's existence will come into question: be ready for it.

Kotler's words are echoed and emphasized by Jim Champy. 'Functions such as marketing, service and finance will not drive the organization of tomorrow. Even business processes will not drive the organization of tomorrow: the market will drive the organization of tomorrow.'

He goes on, 'here's why. In the next fifteen years, the whole purpose of many organizations will come into question. Publishers, retailers, banks, entertainment companies, software companies – many industries – are about to reconfigure in fundamental ways.'

And Champy warns tomorrow's executive cadre that they must be careful to ask the right questions of themselves. 'The first question for managers to ponder in such companies is not "how can we out-market the competition or provide better customer service?" With information technology enabling radical changes in processes (which is what re-engineering is all about) and now transforming whole products and industries, the key question becomes "what business are we really in and how can we uniquely provide value to customers as our product and processes change dramatically?" Such a marketplace focus will drive everything else – what business we decide to be in, what processes in that business we decide to re-engineer and how to re-engineer them.'

The Economist Intelligence Unit's landmark study, 'The Successful Corporation of the Year 2000' also touts the customer as the key, saying, 'the customer will continue to be king. Firms will accept this philosophy not as a functional matter, but as a way of driving the majority of business decisions across all functions.'

The survey noted that 'Japanese corporations have long since shifted from total quality management's zero-defect policy – and are currently moving even further to a philosophy of "quality that surprises".'

However, that might apply to some Japanese companies – but not all. Consultant and author, T.W. Kang, observes, 'In high-tech industries, marketing must drive the organization; specifically marketing must determine and forecast customer needs, which requires a strong input into technology and product development.'

But, he suggests that, 'there are those – particularly in Japan – who believe in manufacturing *über alles*, but what good is it to be building inventory in items that are not wanted by the market?'

So, even in Japan it seems that there are those who find the idea of change difficult to grasp fully. But perhaps what they don't fully realize is that the business world has already moved into a position where the winners and losers of tomorrow have virtually already been shuffled in the pack or cards.

Indeed a supporting word or two on the all-out focus on the customer comes from Peter Drucker, 'Organizations will be increasingly market driven. That is not the same thing as being customer driven. In fact the most important element in any market are the non-customers, the people who should be customers for the product or service your company produces, but buy from the competition.'

That is subscribing to the idea that you cannot call anyone a customer until they have bought from you twice. Then you can begin to develop a bond between yourselves and them.

John Humble bluntly makes the point that 'if you are not market driven you will just not survive! Every organization – profit or non profit – exists to serve. In a fiercely competitive twenty-first century, the winners will be those that not only satisfy customers but delight them. Not only respond to customer's expressed needs, but deliver satisfactions customers didn't even know existed.'

You must move from market-driven to market driving: anticipating a need before the customers actually know they want it.

Moving to market driving

In an interview with Management Centre Europe several years ago, Philip Kotler anticipated Humble's remark. 'Being market-driven means you're reacting to people's expressed wants and needs, you're just listening and providing. I'd like to see more

Ever closer to the customer

No one – certainly no owner or senior manager – has ever got closer to the customer than Irish supermarket entrepreneur Feargal Quinn. So great is his reputation that executives from all over the globe fly to Dublin where his chain of supermarkets are not just best practice but a shrine to the service ethic.

As the customer becomes the total focus of tomorrow's business, learning from those who know how to make it all work is vital. Moreover, that importance can only increase as the battles for market share erupt.

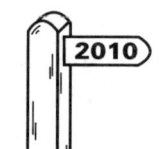 Get out there and try and buy your own products, buy your competitor's products, see what they and you offer from the customer's point of view.

Here's what Feargal Quinn says about getting close to the customer. 'Becoming customer driven is, above all, a question of getting closer to the customer than people in business usually are. Why? Because to make the decisions that will bring your customers back, you need to think like a customer. In the real sense you need to be able to become a customer.

'Few people realize just how difficult this is as the marketplace looks totally different from where the customer is standing. In our business, we have a rule which requires our top management to do their own household shopping once a month. This gives them first-hand experience of what shopping is like from the customer's perspective. When you've stood in a queue for four minutes at a time when you're under pressure to get away, you discover just how long four minutes can be. You see the problem of queuing in a very different light to the one you have when looking at it from a management perspective.

'A word of warning. You may need to work hard to avoid having yourself treated as a VIP. This is precisely what you do not want. Most of your customers are not treated as VIPs. The perspective you want is that of the ordinary customer.

continued

Cuddling up to the customer

> **INSIGHT**
>
> 'There's a certain airline that I travel with quite frequently, and it always amuses me to see how management from the airline get priority treatment from the cabin staff when they travel as passengers. It's not just that I, as a paying customer, feel that the cabin staff's attention should be focused on me and people like me. What really amuses me is that I can see how inaccurate a picture these people are getting of what it's really like to travel on their airline.'

companies moving from being market-driven to market driving, anticipating demands that have yet to be expressed and even creating entirely new demands.'

And he gave the example of one-hour photo processing that, until customers were told it was technically and economically feasible, they expressed no demand for it. 'What was Polaroid, but the answer to another dream people never knew they had – to see a picture the moment after they had taken it.'

N. Venkatraman of Boston University at a top management conference in London in 1994, used Polaroid for a different type of example and one that stresses the strong tug that technology is going to have in the corporation. 'Edward Land was the founder of Polaroid. And what Edward Land did was to instill in the company a vision or a culture that said, "Let's make our products obsolete, before our competitors do." Think about that. It's saying, the moment I introduce a new product I'm going to actively try to make that product obsolete, because I know the competitive advantage is only sustained if I know what the next generation of product is going to be. So you should ask yourself the question: "can you make your processes obsolete before your competitors do?" '

Venkatraman also points tomorrow's manager towards the idea that the customer rules and that sloppy service is not going to be rewarded anymore. For many of us in Europe, who have waited months for a phone line, his example is particularly apt.

'If I came to your city and I rented an apartment, which already had a telephone line and I brought my own phone with me, how long before I would have a telephone line that is working?' According to a study he carried out, the responses ranged from 15 minutes by one of the US operating companies to three to four weeks in some of the newly industrialized countries. 'But we are becoming a global market-place and we have to ask ourselves the question, when U.S. West or British Telecom or France Telecom start competing in the global market-place they are going to re-define the process by which customers are going to get value. I can no longer say that it is going to take me three weeks after you have made the application to get that telephone line, when the best-in-class is 15 minutes, or in some cases nearly instantaneous.' Someone like that who can compete head to head on your own turf is someone to be concerned about. While it might be excellent news for the consumer it is very bad news for any bloated, bureaucratic business.

Venkatraman uses this example to make it clear that we must 'benchmark what our competitors can do in the market-place. There is no point in re-designing by merely looking at the past. Because re-designing with a historical focus allows you only to rectify yesterday's weaknesses and by that time your competitor has already caught up.'

He asks executives to take on board a very important lesson. 'We are increasingly becoming a global market-place, and it is possible for countries in those economies to actually leap-frog in terms of process performance, by radically exploiting the technology capabilities.'

This means that you can be sitting happily in your organization, feeling safe in the knowledge that a process you have developed is still being sought after by your exasperated competitors, only to discover that a world away, an engineer or a scientist has developed the same capabilities as part of a totally different process. Suddenly from a different part of the globe, most probably from a different industry, a quite possibly a whole lot cheaper a fearsome competitor is born.

Another direction that technology is taking the marketing organization in is the ability to segment into ever smaller niches, to really individualize your offer to the prospective buyer.

One area where this is already making itself felt is an increased sophistication in household buying. This is a definite trend, that according to Philip Kotler, underscores that people 'now have a need to get first-class service, satisfaction, timely delivery and lower costs. The winners will be those who service better, deliver faster and charge less. The major change will be knowing customers in a much richer way.'

While it may be good news for the consumer, the forecasters suggest it is going to be hell for those fighting to offer better and better customer choice. Says Lou Stern, of Northwestern University, 'We can now take the data from 240,000 neighbourhoods in the USA and break these down into differing lifestyle categories. So we end up with niches like "pools and patios", "shotguns and pick-up trucks".'

 There's no middle class anymore, so don't try and cater to it: you'll go out of business.

No middle-class market

Stern is certain that, armed with this much individual data, the market battles of the twenty-first century will be bloody and long, more akin to hand-to-hand combat, 'the battle for market will be neighbourhood by neighbourhood, street by street. There isn't any homogeneous middle-class anymore, they are groups with different lifestyles: it is heterogeneous.'

Failure to see that, riding on a surfeit of choice and competing offers, the middle class in the USA and increasingly in Europe has fragmented into many 'mini-lifestyles' is already chalking up victims on the corporate loser board.

Lester Thurow observes, 'it's called the vanishing middle and the new consumer. If you look at American retailing, the stores that have either gone out of business or are under enormous economic pressure are the middle-class stores. What is the chance, that simply by accident, all the incompetent managers could have been managing middle-class stores? That, of course, is a zero probability event. The middle-class stores are in trouble not because they are badly managed, but because their customers are disappearing. And people are either going downscale to the Walmarts and K-Marts, or upscale to the Bloomingdale's. And the proto-typical middle-class stores like Sears are in trouble.'

Here's what you'll have to do

Philip Kotler has been accepted as the most profound thinker on marketing for a long, long time. So when he gives examples of how companies innovate to get a march on their competitors it might be a good idea to take note. At a recent international marketing conference, Kotler catalogued outstanding examples of the way you can make a difference and get the customer to love you and knock your competitors for six at the same time. All of them show a lot of thought and the development of one good idea. Often it only takes that one good idea to make the difference between a sale and no sale at all.

Remember, innovation, new ideas and speed, all are the drivers of tomorrow and you have to keep re-inventing your product. If you're not doing it now, someone else is. Someone who is going to steal the market share in an already crowded market-place.

Kotler says, 'As customers look for low price, customization, extras and quality, some companies try to "own" one of these things.' Indeed some companies 'try to own a word' like Motorola for quality, Compaq for value, Intel for brand equity, 3M for innovation, IBM for service.

'Think always about your own business,' Kotler advised, 'are you doing anything to honour your customer?'

Here are Kotler's examples of getting close-up to the customer:

- Healthcare giant Baxter give points to clients so hospitals and others can get cash back, get extra goods or buy into consulting services (like waste management and IT).
- ICI's paints division divided their world into four niche groups: consumers, painters, decorators and retailers and figured out a reward strategy for each. Example: if you are a painter in Malaysia and you buy ten cans of paint, ICI offer free work insurance.
- Consultants, Bain & Company give a guarantee that they will not charge fees if they fail the assignment.
- In the USA, Speedy Muffler King give you your money back *and* 10 percent if you don't like the product or the service.
- Pharmaceutical company G.D. Searle, will refund cost of medicines if they are ineffective.

continued

- Auto giant, GM's, greenfield start-up Saturn car division, will take back the car and refund full amount for *any* reason.
- Allied Van Lines have a pledge to give customers $100 for every day they are late with a delivery.
- Canadian upstart supermarket firm, Loblaws guarantee that if you are not happy with *their* cookies or cola they will replace it with Nabisco or Coca-Cola.
- The Savoy Hotel in London gives a free limousine service to the airport (both ways). It is cheaper than price cuts, but the perceived value is high.
- Virgin Airlines became the bane of British Airways by innovative ideas. They will measure you for a suit on the plane and it is ready when you get to Hong Kong and they serve ice-cream and popcorn when the in-flight movie starts.
- Nestlé's baby foods operation sponsors baby change and feed stops on French autoroutes.
- Luxury car-maker Lexus did a deal with the Sydney Opera House. If you drive up in a Lexus (and only a Lexus) the doorman will park your car and there will be a glass of champagne waiting for you.
- Spanish porcelain maker Lladro founded a collector's society and organizes special cultural tours of Spain.
- The Swatch company created a collector's club with 100,000 members. Issues special 'limited' editions that members bid for, creating artificial scarcity.

Kotler warned his audience that they must, 'think how you would react if you were the competitors. It's like a tennis game – if you hit the ball, someone is going to hit it back and you have to hit it back again.'

Another important factor about being the innovator: doing it first is fun; playing catch-up is hard work.

All these examples were given in mid-1940.

A good example of how changing lifestyle needs can change a market completely, but also provide rich pickings for those smart enough to recognize it is provided by Philip Kotler.

He talks of how Harley-Davidson, which not too long ago was written off as having being out manoeuvred by the Japanese, revitalized itself to become a market winner. 'Harley-Davidson is not selling a motorcycle – it sells a lifestyle. And it's not the lifestyle for the toughs on the streets who wear black leather jackets, but for executives. Most Harley fans are executives, who on Sunday shed their business suits, put on boots and black leather jackets, put on temporary tattoos and get on their motorcycle. They go to a retail store called Harley's where they can drink Harley beer, and in New York there is a restaurant called Harley's. That's lifestyle. That company reinvented itself, like I think Richard Branson [of Virgin Atlantic] is re-inventing the flying experience.'

Learn to love demanding customers

But Kotler says that we always have to be cautious how we deal with our customers and the first thing to do is make sure we have tough ones to deal with. Why do we want tough customers? Because they set the standards for everyone else. 'Always, always serve some of your most demanding customers and don't worry about making money on them. The fact that they are demanding will train you in such a way you will make money on all the other customers.'

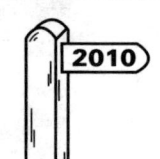 Look and learn from your most demanding customer. They'll teach you more about your product than anyone else.

Michael Porter strongly supports Kotler's view of keeping a few lions that need taming in the corporate sales cage to keep teaching yourself how to serve the tough customers. 'Every company should know and be selling to the most demanding customer for your product: the customer with the toughest needs, the one who is most knowledgeable about the product, the one who is the most sophisticated about using the product.'

Echoing Kotler he adds, 'You might not make a single nickel of profit selling to them, but that is one of the ways your

> **A word about complacency**
>
> Harvard's Ted Levitt, whose ideas and books pioneered much of what we take for granted in the marketing sphere today, set the scene for the next millennium in an interview some years ago on how to sustain success.
>
> According to Levitt's view there were five rules for young companies to remember, if they were to survive, to get old, fat and rich. Today they apply to us all.
>
> - The first thing you have to realize is that the customer is fickle. Customer loyalty does not exist, they will go wherever they get more for their money.
> - Many young companies fail because they cannot control success – or because they don't really understand their market.
> - Defining a market need, starting a business and bringing it up to speed are easy; the really difficult part is to have sustained growth and to constantly renew your offering in the face of competition and changing consumer demands.
> - Once you've created something that works, competitors will learn from your mistakes and improve on what you're offering.
> - Remember, no one's smarter than the market. So don't try to change the market – follow it. And, if you think you're successful, don't believe your own advertising – that's how most businesses fail.

organization is going to progress. If you have a big internal debate with your people on how to improve a product you are going to have a lot of debate. But if you have this guy who is a customer saying that you guys stink, that cuts through a lot of the sacred cows of the company. That is the kind of thing that is going to determine which companies win and which companies lose.'

John Humble adds to this, 'quality in the objective sense of meeting agreed specifications will cease to be an advantage and will become the entry price for joining in the competitive game. Measuring customer satisfaction will become as respected and professional as today's financial systems.

Service excellence will become the test for every key management decision. It will become increasingly recognized that there are no slick solutions to better service. A holistic approach, which integrates customers, systems and the company staff is necessary.'

To ensure this happens, enterprises of the next millennium must put programmes in place to give their executives what Porter calls, 'a deeply ingrained understanding of how to meet customer needs that will require a much more sophisticated management tool-kit'.

One man who is intent on giving his managers an on-going lesson in dealing with the customer is Pier Carlo Falotti, President and CEO of AT&T Europe, Africa, Middle East. Falotti, who cut his teeth on giving superior customer service during his tenure as European supremo of Digital Equipment, has long subscribed to the concept of the market dictating the business offering.

Falotti's viewpoint is simple and direct, the customer is the end result of all the thinking and all the action that the organization does – every single day.

Ask yourself this: 'will a customer be willing to pay for what I have done today?' If the answer is 'no', perhaps you're doing things wrong.

Falotti's idea is that, 'Too many organizations are designed to fit their own needs, not those of the customer'. He says, 'What you should think of – all the time – is "will a customer be willing to pay for what I have done today?" If the answer is "no", then you had better question what you are doing in that job.'

Additionally, as highly empowered, flexible teams will be as dominant in the corporation of the future, Falotti sees that an ability to work along with others is going to be a distinguishing factor. 'I don't want to have people who just have satisfaction if they score a goal: I want the team to win the match. If we let the people who are supposed to do the scoring make the goals, and we give them the support they need, then we can all enjoy winning.'

Have an obsession with speed

Theo Lieven is the founder and chairman of Vobis, an upstart German computer retailer and manufacturer based in Aachen that has now become Europe's biggest retailer of PCs almost entirely on its ability to innovate and compete against anyone on price and speed to market. They got into manufacturing when their traditional suppliers couldn't get them products fast enough to meet demand in their retail stores.

Lieven has a self-confessed obsession with speed to the market and here he explains how that also means lower prices to make it, which result in lower prices to the consumer.

'Flexibility and speed are the words that define our organization. Flexibility and speed belong together. With low speed you cannot be flexible.

'We don't need five years to design a product – a computer takes six or nine months for most manufacturers – far less for us.'

Lieven explains the Vobis strategy as follows. 'It goes like this. A new development evolves in computer hardware. Let us say it will be ready for shipment from the Far East in nine months' time. Computer manufacturers see an opportunity for a new product based on this improvement. So they put their ideas together and start the process of new product development.

'IBM might need a lead time of nine months to develop and introduce a new computer, they have to start buying the components immediately. Compaq might need only three months lead time, so they can start buying in six months' time. And they get maybe a 20 percent better price for the components than IBM.

'At Vobis we only need three weeks. We start buying in eight months, and we get maybe a 30 percent better price than IBM.

'It might seem that Vobis is always cheaper than the others, but we aren't cheaper – we are faster, we are closer to the market.'

Accountable entrepreneurism

Accountable entrepreneurism seems to drive Falotti's organizational model, 'If you work as a taxi driver – as a small entrepreneur – you don't check with your boss what you should do – you haven't got one!

That is why I believe in delayering the organization so we can all get down to the level of the customer. We must take out the layers that create filters for information and be more timely in our actions, in the way we respond. If you are going to school for customer service it's too late.'

What Falotti and other intelligent, forward thinking managers are advocating is: get thinking all the time about your customers, fulfil their needs and the rest follows.

Even more importantly they are telling all of us that we must keep changing our vision, changing our offering. In this new game of business roulette, where lots of change gets a high approval rating, switching from red to black and back again is not a wild strategy, it's an imperative.

In their highly acclaimed book *Competing for the Future*, Gary Hamel and C.K. Prahalad give a list of seven very useful questions that any executive should be asking, not once, but very frequently. Buy their book and learn their views on what the competition is going to do with the laggards in any and every industry. But also carry these questions with you, in your wallet, in your purse, and take them out and try and answer them as often as possible.

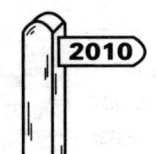 Get thinking all the time about your customers, fulfil their needs and the rest follows.

As we said in the opening to this chapter, none of this is unique, what it takes is a lot of dedication to getting it right and the ability to have the right sort of people to follow it all through.

Just to show that understanding the market and knowing what the customer is like is something we should all have been doing a lot more of for a long time. Here's Peter Drucker talking about another great management icon, Alfred Sloan, of General Motors: 'Sloan would disappear from Detroit the first week of every quarter. He'd leave behind him a sealed envelope to be opened only in the event of his wife's death. Still at seventy he would go to a GM dealer and ask if he could work for a week as a car salesman or in the service department.'

Sloan knew what some people still have to learn, you have to be on the outside, that's where the customers are. But Drucker points out that, for today's organization it isn't quite as simple as that and you should always keep in mind that there are several outsides.

'One is the people who buy. Two is the people you want to recruit. Three is the outside of money. I am always appalled at the chief financial officer's ignorance of the market, they believe the bank will tell them, but you have to be out to find out.'

Finally, Drucker warns that you only get to know about technology when you really see what it can do first hand. 'Technology doesn't work how they say it should, also technologies are criss-crossing. Totally different technologies are coming together, they change everyday, and you have to be on the outside to see what is happening.'

Great marketers shape needs, poor marketers respond to needs that are already there.

As marketing's champion, and the man who has recorded many of its successes and failures, a last point from Philip Kotler: 'No one expects a marketing team to come up with a permanently winning idea. Venerable products and brands will collapse as new things come along and offer better value.'

'Remember, good marketing is responding; great marketing is shaping needs.'

As more and more companies change their total focus to the customer, shaping those needs, innovating to meet expectations cannot be seen anymore as something exceptional, just a way of doing business as usual. All of us who expect to be around in 15 years are just going to have to make marketing our way of doing our daily business. For many of us this might

What about alliances?

One area that needs a lot closer examination in this market-ruled organization is alliances. Although some firms seem to have been able to make alliances work quite well, others have had a very bad time of it. Indeed, the consensus is, before you get in, make sure you know exactly what you are going to get out of it. More important, is giving away some of your ideas, secrets and processes really worth what you are going to gain?

Warning signal: Make sure you know exactly what *you* want to get out of an alliance and go for it ... don't jump too far, too fast.

Michael Porter says that 'supplier/customer relationships and new partnership arrangements have helped in introducing new technologies, but I think we are probably at the peak of alliance fever: so many companies have had a low success rate and in a world of change it is an unstable way to work.'

Management commentator and business school professor, Liam Fahey agrees and warns companies who might see an alliance as a quick way into a market to be careful. During an interview for a Management Centre Europe project on new management ideas, he said, 'firms are entering into a wide range of alliances and joint ventures. This will result sometimes not in a quick death in the market-place but in a slow, tortuous death over a number of years as a firm's capability is gradually hooked away from it. You give away your technology, you give away your distinctive capability – and where do you end up?'

That, perhaps, is a over gloomy scenario. Many management commentators feel that unless you provoke and proactively search for alliances you won't be able to develop needed technology of new ideas as a stand-alone corporation. Furthermore, as the line between what a company and its key suppliers blurs and we begin to see the emergence of the real boundaryless corporation, there will – almost certainly – have to be a place for alliances.

continued

> **INSIGHT**
>
> Possibly the skills required to effectively manage alliances and ever closer links with suppliers and/or customers is one of the things that has been missing so far. Perhaps forward-thinking management should put learning to manage alliances – effectively – at the top of the training and development agendas.

be difficult, but we have to be able to see our organization, our products, our services the way they are perceived by the customer. Without our ability to do that we will see a gradual slide of our market as others come up with better answers and better responses.

But there is something else we should keep in mind: the leaders in the marketplace will always be able to pull off something exceptional – something we never thought of, something the others can't do that delights the customer. They will be the winners.

What to watch for

- Above all become the customer. Get to think about your job or your business the way they do. If you're not adding value to your business, think about how you are going to change.
- Be aware of the dangers of complacency. Innovation and speed are for always, not an option.
- The way to a customer's purse is doing something, creating something, providing something they didn't know they wanted. Anticipate needs with quality that surprises: then do it again and again.
- Don't get hooked on alliances because they seem an easy way into a market. Check out the real motives of your possible partners and don't give away your hard won advantages unless there is a very exceptional return.
- All the same don't throw the idea of alliances out, they are going to be in demand. Learn the necessary skills to manage alliances to your advantage.

- Look into your business, or your job and assess honestly how redundant it is now and in the future. As the future shape of whole industries comes into question, ask yourself if where you are now is where you want to be.
- Successful companies are already moving from being market driven to market driving (anticipating those customer needs and fulfilling them). Is your organization doing that? If not, should you be a part of it?
- Don't hate the demanding customer, the complainer, the one who keeps you awake at night. Learn to love them. If you can please them, you can more than please everyone else.

7
Managing the technology of a new millennium

> There aren't any rules here, we are trying to get something done.
>
> *Thomas Edison*

The way we are going with technology, by 2010 practically anything is possible. If we look back at the last twenty years, we can see that we are multiplying our technological abilities at an ever increasing rate. There is little doubt that technology will spawn new businesses, just as it will change traditional businesses out of all recognition. In doing so it will also change the way we work forever. By the next century hardware and software will be so sophisticated that we probably won't have to get out of bed to go to work. In the world of 2010 no one will ever have the excuse that the alarm didn't go off. Wherever our 'office' will be, information technology (IT) will drive our management structures totally.

People will be embracing technology in a different way, just as the present generation was changed by television. Think about it this way, a thirty-five-year-old in 2010 is twenty-years-old today. A thirty-year-old multi-tasking specialist executive is just fifteen. In twenty years' time when the present executive generation comes to retire, the company they leave will have in it executives that are ten-years-old right now. Imagine all the technology they will absorb over that period between now and then. Also imagine how second nature it will be to them.

As a writer, lecturer and consultant, Mike Kami has always been at the cutting edge of technology. In fact in the dim distant past, Kami was part of the IBM team that came up with the – then revolutionary – golf ball typewriter; a piece of technology that seems today about as significant and useful as a horse and cart.

 Are you carrying a computer with you? Get used to the habit now, you'll need it tomorrow.

Ever since the computer's appearance in a user-friendly format, Kami has been urging executives to start using them. Ten years ago he was asking at his ever-popular top management seminars, 'how many of you have your computer with you?' Usually the answer was none.

Communication is no longer an option

But Kami points out that for the world of tomorrow, communication is no longer an option, no longer a gadget 'it will be the mental extension of a person. It must be considered a part of you. Let's face it, Clinton learned about the war in Iraq from CNN not the CIA. If you haven't learned from that by now, you have a problem. If you are not 100 times smarter than you were ten years ago you don't count anymore and you should retire right now. Remember, tomorrow's executives will have no problem with technology as they will have been brought up with it.'

Consultant and author, John Humble, who started his professional career when computers were the size of a house and fawned over by white-coated technicians, has watched the developments of technology and their impact on management for over four decades.

'Today it is impossible to imagine any organization where information technology is not crucially important for success and to support this an entirely new corps of professional IT managers have developed.

'Lean production can now produce small numbers of customized products at phenomenal speed and quantity, often creating new relationships with suppliers and customers that is in itself another IT-driven revolution; mass production has been irrevocably turned upside-down.'

As Humble says, all of this has major implications for those who will manage the corporations of the future. According to him, there are six important lessons that we have to learn – and learn well – before we can really create the technologically driven corporation.

Search for the real competition

Consultant and author, John Humble talks frequently about the problems of making radical change in an organization that considers itself successful. What he calls the 'why ruin a winning line' syndrome. Or as some of us remember the old consultant's advice – that sadly some companies still embrace as the divine organizational truth – 'if it ain't broke don't fix it'. As we all now know, the time to fix it is all the time – in this fast-paced world there's no merit in waiting.

While that may already be the success recipe for 2010, Humble points out that in many companies 'sheer inertia, built-in conformity and contempt for competitors are hard to overcome until a company is really threatened.'

And these days the competition can appear from the most unlikely places. Michael Porter, the man who has spent more time studying competitive strategy than anyone else, has a favourite example that can send a collective shiver down any organization's spine. What it illustrates is that, even if you yourself are innovating, someone else can be doing things in a different way using newly available technology – in a way you have never considered.

Porter says, 'Canada has been the largest exporter of newsprint. Why does Canada have that advantage? Because Canada has immense, gigantic forestry reserves. There are just so many trees up there that anywhere you look you just swing an axe and a tree falls down. That was the big competitive advantage in the post-war period. But what's happened is that all of a sudden we've learned how to make high quality newsprint out of recycled paper. All of a sudden the Canadians are in deep trouble, because instead of having a rural forest where you go out and cut some trees, now what you need to be an efficient newsprint producer is an urban forest, which is the place where they produce lots of recycled paper. So the newsprint plants are going up near metropolitan areas, in densely populated areas. Technology has rendered Canada's advantage obsolete.'

So think what could happen in your industry. Somewhere down that road to 2010 is there a rock for you to trip over?

- As the costs of systems escalate (already capital investment in IT far outweighs all other areas), and poorly planned systems may, literally, put the business at risk, it is vital to analyse needs and choices with ever greater professional stringency. That elusive partnership between technical experts and general managers *must* be forged.
- Modern IT systems do not work well in the classic command and control pyramid. Flattened structures are essential.
- Knowledge is power. Middle managers in particular have always been reluctant to share information. Now, with most people in an organization with a computer terminal at their fingertips, the invisible power structures change totally.
- The sharply defined boundaries of one organization are no longer an operational reality. For example, a just-in-time delivery system inextricably links a company's suppliers into an IT web.
- IT also bring unheard of entrepreneurial opportunities for new businesses. For example, motor insurance firms and banks without any premises, who use phone and modem links are beginning to take a significant share of the market from traditional suppliers.
- Modern information systems have huge potentials for sharing knowledge and extending the learning process. Wherever you are in the world you can access the past experience of others and learn from it.

George Day, a professor at the Wharton School still sees problems in getting executives to embrace IT, despite all the trend signs, that if you don't you will be left behind. 'It is still troublesome to get managers to appreciate IT's power and usefulness – the average manager has still not figured this out. the IT specialist yes, the others, no.'

Agreeing strongly that this is still an issue, Peter Drucker suggests that 'most executives today are computer literate, albeit on a very low level as a rule, comparable perhaps to the reading

 We are all going to be out of date very fast. Expect to go back to school every three years.

literacy of an eight-year-old. Tomorrow, executives will have to be information-literate and very few understand the challenge.'

Drucker goes on to say that the information revolution has not yet been fully exploited, but that it is something that we must do as we run up to 2010. 'What it requires is that the executives think through what information they need on what, in what form, from whom and when. It equally requires them to think through what information they owe, to whom, in what form, what time span and so on. So far practically no one has done this and the Management Information System has been no help at all.'

To keep up with the bounties that the information revolution will bring, Drucker points out that, 'executives tomorrow will have to accept that they will have to continue to learn and learn not only on the job, but in any number of formal learning processes, whether a Management Centre Europe seminar, a university course or a software program.'

The obsolescence of knowledge

'Tomorrow there will be knowledge workers – there are very few of them today. And knowledge will become obsolete incredibly fast. After three years a knowledge worker has to go back to school.'

As companies begin facing the challenge of turning staff into true knowledge workers, this of course has major implications for the re-engineering process. Re-engineering's champion, Jim Champy, comments, 'One way to look at the re-engineering phenomenon is to say that re-engineering is about how information technology is enabling entirely new, efficient and effective business processes. A host of technologies that are just becoming affordable and practical – interactive multimedia, groupware, wireless communications, to name a few – will become technology "platforms" of the re-engineered processes for the rest of the 1990s.'

'So we'll continue to do a substantial amount of 'process' re-engineering for the foreseeable future. More fundamentally, we'll see 'industry' re-engineering, as IT begins to redefine the once clear lines that separated many industries. For example, will the electronic news source of the future be controlled by today's newspaper publishers? By today's broadcasters? By America Online? By Microsoft? Or by some upstart information provider?

> **Countries too must compete**
>
> Harvard Business School's, Michael Porter makes a telling point about technology, when he explains that it has wiped out much of the traditional advantages we thought we had. And he uses not a company but a country example – which also serves to remind us that without collective responses that bind companies, industries and countries or regions together, winning the business battles of the next century will be almost impossible.
>
> Porter says, 'We all know that Japan has very high cost of land. You would think that high cost would render the Japanese uncompetitive, but clearly it doesn't. One of the reasons it doesn't is because the Japanese have been incredibly imaginative in using technology to reduce demand for space. That is what the just-in-time thing was all about. It was not about quality: it was about not having inventory sitting around on your factory floor.'

As the news product becomes an electronically delivered one it's not clear who the players will be.

'So information technology is going to reinvent a number of industries. I'd expect the media, retailing, banking and insurance to be hit first.'

Harvard's Michael Porter also expects some major changes in both the way we do business and the businesses themselves. As we move toward 2010 he believes that we will enter 'a new technology era, where IT will transform organizations'.

He is sure that IT specialists won't continue to dominate, as managers 'will be able to create their own software' it will be so user-friendly. And, for the benefit of any people who think this only applies to traditionally focused high-tech industries and these changes don't involve them, he adds, 'There are no low-tech industries. Hauling trash, a temporary agency, they all can – and will – be improved.'

Don't delegate technology decisions

And he emphasizes the point that we must learn the lesson that 'we cannot delegate technology to the technologist. The good manager must understand the technological requirements of the business.'

Information technology is not a specialization anymore ...it is a part of everyone's decision-making process.

This challenge not to leave IT decisions and developments to the technical specialists is a point frequently hammered home by N. Venkatraman of Boston University. 'There must be a shift in the mind-set, where IT is not something that people do in the basement, in a technologist's domain. It is not! It is a fundamental business capability. We need to align our business vision with the IT vision and in some cases the technology vision might drive what your business capabilities might be in the future. It is a shared management responsibility between business managers and technologists and we need both of them to work together. Technologists realize the technology potential but not the business context, business managers understand value delivery but they don't understand technology. The new business vision is shaped by IT capabilities, but ultimately it is a management challenge.'

It may in the final analysis be a management challenge, but tomorrow's executives are going to need help. Competition these days increasingly comes from new quarters and, more importantly new countries. So it isn't just the management team who need to be aware. Industries and governments need to make investments to ensure that they themselves – and the businesses that support their industrial base – are continuously competitive. The market of tomorrow in many cases is just a few key strokes and half a world away. Quicker than going to the next street, never mind the next town.

To illustrate his concerns, and to underline that management must start embracing new technologies for themselves soon, N. Venkatraman points to the fact that 'the biggest software producing operations today are in Bangalore, India. Why? Because it is possible for me to connect and monitor the operations of the software designers and programmers in Bangalore whether I am sitting in London or Paris or anywhere. You've got to create the organizational process that allows managers to create value from the technology that they could not conceive of a few years back.'

Bolstering Champy's message of radical design, he continues, 'the increased benefits that you are going to get from technology requires you to radically re-design the organization: relative to your competitors, relative to the new entrants that could compete with you in the future.'

And Venkatraman is sure that new technology is going to let us do more than just manage the office more efficiently than ever before. It will drastically speed up development times and the invention of new processes as well. 'It is also possible to design new products across time zones. Many pharmaceutical companies, many automotive companies, many other companies who have R&D labs are electronically linked between the USA, Europe and Japan so they can create a twenty-four-hour development cycle. So, if you are creating teams, make the teams cut across time boundaries as well as organizational boundaries. That is the way we are going to get benefits that we haven't seen in the twentieth century. That is going to be the hallmark of successful innovators in the twenty-first century.'

Like Venkatraman, consultant and author, T.W. Kang sees IT as opening up countless possibilities for firms in the new millennium. 'Just in the same way that we could not imagine that the electronic calculator could become as thin as a credit card, so – by extrapolating into the future – we are likely to vastly underestimate what technology will do. After some gestation period, multimedia technology will change the way we buy and sell products for ever. For example we will be able to purchase a house through a detailed multiple listing service without actually having to visit it.'

But Kang sees a few downsides as well, 'There will be confusion and stress associated with this. Imagine that your boss can get in touch with you on an airplane right after you've had that long deserved cocktail!'

The mobile office

Liam Fahey of Babson College and Cranfield School of Management, says that we are in danger of creating a 'class of management bedouins. You don't need people coming

> **INSIGHT**
>
> **E-mail it**
>
> This book was written in Brussels and Spain. During that process the text was constantly electronically transferred between the two places and also to many of the people who read the manuscript. Even today, effective use of technology can cut delivery time dramatically and make anywhere in the world your office, as you have access to your files at any time – all it requires is a phone line: you don't even need an overnight courier service.

downtown, by 2010 we will have the truly mobile office and you'll just do the job on the move. We are seeing the creation of a new class of mobile, agile, aggressive people.'

But, despite what has been written about outworking and telecommuting, lots of people don't see the total demise of office life – after all, apart from the home – there would be nothing to make TV shows about.

 All the signs show that working from home – except for some exceptions – just won't happen.

Some fear that being forced to work from home could be a back door route to redundancy, while others who have taken up teleworking complain of loneliness and feeling out of touch.

A report in *The Financial Times* concluded that, 'there are virtually no technological barriers, no legal barriers, no cost barriers to having people working from home – the barriers are human ones.'

The truth of it is – and this is how we will ultimately solve how we settle this dilemma of technology versus social needs – most of us just don't like being on our own for long periods. The idea of not having the 'social' atmosphere of an office environment, fills a lot of people with dread. Additionally, it raises many issues of control and reward that are only now beginning to be looked at.

As former Dean of the Sloan School of Management at MIT, Lester Thurow says, 'We all want to be in one place to get the corporate gossip – no one wants to be a periphery. You also need a godfather, a mentor.' He adds, 'What replaces the HQ? There are a lot of technical possibilities, but sociologically I think it is unlikely to happen. What I think will happen is that a mix will evolve between human contact and technology.'

He suggests that we consider that 'everything we've invented should have spread us out – London and New York shouldn't really exist.'

Thurow uses the analogy of seals, who crowd together on one sandbar, when there's hundreds of empty ones to choose from. 'Humans are just like seals, we like to pile on top of each other.'

Peter Drucker notes that, 'now that idea and information can travel to where people are there is basically no need for the "office". The post Second World War city is an office city – before 1940 there were only two skylines in the world, New York and Chicago. In the Frankfurt in which I worked in 1930 or the Brussels or the London in which I worked a few years later a tall building had four stories – now even hick towns have skyscrapers. They are office skyscrapers and they are already dysfunctional.' But Drucker sides with others that we are unlikely to function as independent, single cell, operations. 'The office of tomorrow will be the headquarters, but I don't believe what's being said that we'll work at home – we like to have companionship.'

Philippe Alloing, European Director Human Resources for A.D. Little in Paris, adds, 'The barrier to people working at home is the desperate need behind the growth of salaried work in modern societies. Namely the obligation to socialize through work as there are no other places to do it.

'The most critical development will be the pretence that worldwide managers can be effective through E-mail, voice mail and wide area tele-conferences.'

But maybe we are beginning to spread out a little. Paul Kahn the CEO of SafeCard Services and former President of AT&T Universal Card says that 'technology is driving a geographical breakdown so you don't need to be in the big cities. Places like Cheyenne, Wyoming or Jacksonville, Florida are small, have less social problems, a five-minute commute, and that is just the start.'

What office technology can we expect?

Executives of 2010 will do their job with an arsenal of high-tech helpers, capable of performing every task from travel reservations, typing a letter or making contact with colleagues and customers. The first generation of these decision support systems exist today and will become more and more a part of 'office' life in the next fifteen years.

The key to many of these new management tools is the neural network. This is a new type of problem-solving computer. Its intelligence comes from 'neural' microchips, which contain replicas of the neurons that make up the human brain.

According to office of the future experts, neural networks will help us surmount several of the crucial barriers where office automation is stalled today. For instance, text and voice recognition and synthesis will be much easier and more accurate with neural-based systems.

A neural network will be so flexible that it will be capable of taking many different forms and be put to a staggering range of uses. When computing, robotics and other related technologies are merged, the resulting systems will essentially be able to 'manage' a business for us, leaving us working time to innovate and develop new ideas as never before.

When can we expect these developments to begin affecting how we work? The specialists are already predicting some dates for breakthrough developments in the office of the future:

- This year (1995): the first computers capable of learning and the first 'vision' programs.
- 2005: the computer keyboard disappears, to be replaced by voice recognition and handwritten character recognition that understands the context of the text.
- 2010: automatic language translation of voice and text.
- 2017: the merging of robotics and neural networking into the first 'baby' computer capable of learning.

The secretaries of the future – or the few that are left by then – become office managers running the technology that runs the office. But, after 2005, there's no excuse any more for all those executives who have shied away from using computers on the grounds that they can't type fast!

Kahn also points out that the technology revolutions ability to let people work from home means that you don't need to lose valuable people, because they cannot get to work. 'Technology allows women to have children and stay at home.'

The rise of the office cluster

Peter Drucker says that, 'more and more people will work in office clusters, working close to where they live, rather than commute to the big city. This trend has already gone quite far in the USA and is beginning in Europe. It is even actually beginning in Japan. It is not so much that we have the technology, we could have done this probably even forty years ago when we only had the telephone. But with telephones, closed circuit vision, fax machines, modems and what have you, the technology has made it clear – even to the least observant – that there is no reason except habit to commute in overcrowded trains into London, New York, Frankfurt and what have you.'

Corporate strategist, John Elkins agrees with Thurow and Alloing that technology might free us to work in different places, but we won't give up our office life completely. 'The concept of the lone eagle may be true, but that requires a very specific, very special attitude. People are social animals, and they won't spend time doing lonely work as some people once thought. Maybe part of the time, but there is a real need for congregation and communal action.'

Elkins also suggests that we don't expect too much or get too concerned with where technology might take us. 'Technology will never go as far as we think – it will constantly be pulled back to be acceptable to society.'

Lou Stern of Northwestern University concurs with Elkins, pointing out that there will be systems to stop any abuses. 'As long as corporations use data to meet my needs that will be fine, but there will be ways to track down those that misuse it.'

Additionally, the sophistication of systems will be so great that safeguards will be built-in to ensure that 'departing' employees or contracted staff will not be able to take your secrets with them. However, this still remains one of the most contentious issues of a truly mobile, educated workforce. Can you ever totally stop abuses of confidential information? As one manager puts it, 'the only consolation in a world where innovation is so fast would be that by the time your secrets were used by a competitor they would already be out of date.'

Technology for everyone

Stern is also fairly certain that concerns about the 'elitism' of the IT revolution will be unfounded. 'The IT revolution is not a corporate solution but a chip solution. Of course inner city kids will get to use it, it will be omnipresent – down the phone line, through your television, so I don't see it creating any sort of polarity in society.' Rather it is going to turn up new uses, new markets, unthought of products and services. The innovator will once more reap the rewards.

As IT systems simplify further, computer illiterates will leap-frog over today's users.

Outplacement consultant Win Nystrom agrees, 'The computer illiterate may find themselves pleasantly leap-frogging the hackers as keyboards succumb to voice-driven administrative and process control systems. There is no doubt that the technology will be targeted and priced for general consumption. On the business front, those technologies that allow us to spend more time 'talking' with our customers or more quality time with our colleagues to give added value solutions for those customers will flourish. They will be indispensable. The limits of that technology are far beyond our present conception, but certainly what will be available and acceptable for "talking" will go beyond multimedia imagery.'

These concerns that we cannot just throw away the office, because it does more than just provide a place for doing business also feature in Richard Pascal's view of tomorrow. 'I'm not sure if an electronic network solves the problems of communicating. I think the reason you are hearing so much talk about community these days is because as work becomes more distributed people have a more tenuous relationship with a long-term employer – not only where they are working but how they are working – and their sense of security is changing. There's a feeling that there's something missing from the human

The fourth generation office

Significant improvements in productivity motivation and costs savings can be made in any office, provided management is smart enough to let it happen.

As we head towards the next millennium, experiments are taking place to build the fourth generation office, the 'space' that every executive will occupy in 2010. The first generation was simply the first office; in the second generation each employee/manager had their own office; in the third generation offices became open plan. That third generation was planned to encourage communication, but in fact it failed miserably, giving too much noise and stress to allow for good productivity.

To develop the fourth generation office, specialists are looking at issues like the best noise level for retentive reading, the best lighting to scan a difficult report, what type of computer screen is the best to work at?

Digital Equipment have already – and successfully – built a working prototype of the fourth generation office at their facility in Finland. Realizing that they had one of the world's most modern IT networks that linked 120,000 people – but they still worked with an office procedure that existed fifty years ago – Digital managers let a sixty-person department develop a space where it could operate to maximum efficiency.

After early attempts to work with an architect failed, the sixty-person team developed the office concept together with no management guidelines.

In this fourth generation office there are people pacing the rooms with cordless phones, reading or consulting a computer screen from the comfort of a reclining chair, or discussing projects over a cup of coffee in a relaxation room. A few way-out features that also work in this microcosm of tomorrow is a corner with garden furniture and a garden swing for meetings of up to four people.

'Hot-desking' offices with only ten places for twenty people, are already operational. The theory: if you are out there visiting customers you don't need a desk and chair every day.

continued

> There are thirty-five work-spaces for the sixty people, with no assigned desks (this is known as 'hot-desking') and management sits in the same rooms, not hidden away.
>
> According to Digital the unique feature is not the physical layout but the fact that the concept revolves around communication and flexibility. First, the sales and service people should be visiting customers, not sitting at desks, so you don't need one desk per person. Second, people in the office should be communicating not tied to their desk because their phone is there (when it was built it was the world's biggest installation of portable phones). Third, people like to work in different environments so there are meeting rooms, traditional desk space and lounge areas. Each employee works in the way they are most comfortable.
>
> This type of fourth generation office is known as a 'free address' facility. How people work is secondary to the company's main goals, that sales targets are being met and business is profitable. According to the experts, savings – including those on real estate costs – from free address offices range between 25 and 40 percent.
>
> For the next millennium, whether they like it or not, management in many of the traditional status-ridden industries like banking and insurance will have to change their way of thinking and play by a new set of rules.
>
> Too many companies are still ruled by the status of the corner office and a work environment that encourages employees to look like they are working, rather than being genuinely productive. In the office of tomorrow that just won't be an issue.

experience, called community. and I think that is going to become more pronounced and I don't think that the network addresses it. Yes I think there will be people working independently, or quasi-independently and I think that the relationship – both the physical relationship as well as the psychological and emotional relationship – in the core organizations will probably diminish. I wouldn't say it will be completely that way, but I think that trend will continue, although I would see some points of social contact, possibly a network of smaller offices spread around so people are not purely relying on IT for contact.'

It seems logical that few see the total demise of office life. If we are to build organizations that owe their success and longevity more to their culture than anything else, the inability of people to share face-to-face ideas and experiences would seem to go against what we are trying to build. Those shared values that are held up as the new corporate glue, cannot properly be communicated through a modem or a video screen. Whether we still head up to the city each day, or drop in to our local 'office cluster' to socialize and find out what's really going on, all of us will need that human contact. With so much technology around, we may find that we need more contact in the future rather than less.

For let's face up to it, so far no one has come up with a way to truly motivate the unseen, lonely tele-commuter and perhaps no one really wants to try that hard. Eventually it comes down to individuals working in a way that makes them do their best and feel good about what they are doing. Enjoying the environment you work in is – although often forgotten – a key part in getting the best out of people – that looks set to continue.

What to watch for

- Get ready for the fourth generation office. It will save on space and running costs, and provide a 'centre' for the far-flung company to meet and exchange ideas.
- IT will drive the office of the future, so you will have to keep investing in equipment and in your own ability to use it.
- Message to top management: IT must not be a mystery department anymore, hidden in the basement. It has to be a central part of the strategic management process.
- IT re-invents business, spawns new businesses and changes others out of all recognition. Take some time and think how IT could impact the way you do your job or run your business.
- Knowledge workers, with the ability to remain up to date will be the middle managers of tomorrow.
- Working from home won't take off. People will need the interaction of face-to-face human contact. But there will continue to be a move away from major conurbations to towns and cities that boast better all-round quality of life.

8

The new covenant for 2010

'I told that girl that my prospects were good
she said baby, it's understood
working for peanuts is all very fine
but I can show you a better time'
> Lennon/McCartney 'Baby You Can Drive My Car' Lennon & McCartney, 1965

If the only tool you have is a hammer, you see every problem as a nail.
> Abraham Maslow

As we have heard constantly throughout the chapters of this book, there is one very *big* item on the agenda of change that affects all of us, no matter where we are in the corporate hierarchy – the job for life has gone. Not only is there no longer a secure berth for Mr or Ms Smith in accounts or order processing, there isn't one for a senior vice-president either: all of us are vulnerable. If the job hasn't fallen victim to new technology and been downsized and mechanized, it has probably been outsourced.

The views of the management thinkers and commentators may differ on exactly how the new-look deal between employer and employee will work; but they all agree that it is going to happen. By 2010, all of us will be in a different world, where employment isn't something you take for granted anymore. The downside is a loss of permanence for those who need that security blanket. The upside will be variety, opportunity and reward for those who want to take it.

Richard Pascale's view of our transition to 2010 looks like this. 'I think what has historically been the role of management is largely – not entirely – going to disappear. A lot of people who had employment as managers ten or twenty years ago are going to have employment doing something else as a player, participant, on teams or as contracted experts. But they will not be in the classic management role nearly to the degree we have needed in the past. I mean the people in Motorola always say management is dead as a profession. I think that is an overstatement, but it is directionally correct.'

How dead management is probably depends on how you define management, and particularly the definition of management in the future. If you take previous statements that middle managers will become specialists or knowledge workers and the managers who are left will have to become executives, as they won't have any power over the people they work with, then the manager of the command and control management process is, definitely dead: within a few years at least. And now that the so-called contract between employer and employee has been torn up, isn't this a good time to not only redefine the job of business executives and specialists, but put new labels — that fit the new working world — onto them?

Just how much any real 'contract' existed between employer and employee is doubted by Peter Drucker. 'If there ever was a contract between employer and employee it has disappeared. In fact in most cases there was no such thing. Employees, including senior executives, were forced to be "loyal" out of fear that they had no more liquidity — and this was true, even in that most mobile of countries, the USA. There is no longer employment security anywhere — it has gone even in Japan.'

Earning employee trust

Continuing, Drucker suggests that now, with all contracts void, the advantage is no longer with the company. 'Companies will have to earn whatever trust an employee, whether a blue collar worker or a senior vice-president, is willing to extend to them. Conversely, employees and especially knowledge workers, will have to think through — and think through very carefully — what the organization should hold them accountable for in the way of contribution and results.'

 Ask yourself this: 'what do I get paid for? Is it the right thing for me? Am I delivering value?'

And Drucker points the way to the questions we will all have to ask ourselves. 'Every manager of tomorrow will have to ask himself at least once a year: What am I getting paid for? Is it the right thing for me? Do I deliver?'

T.W. Kang agrees that the Japanese dream of full employment has soured and will require some other system for the next millennium. 'There is no doubt that the contract is broken. In Japan, where the bond between employer and employee has been one of the strongest in the world, there is talk every day about favouring performance over security and seniority. In the twenty-first century there is likely to be something called a 'portfolio' career – something like the consultants of today. He or she will take her portfolio of skills and experience and may even be able to market it to several non-competing companies at the same time.'

Jim Champy explains that the new methods are not an option, 'The old contract will have to be redefined. The reason is that a job for life, or even a job for good performance, will be an albatross around the neck of companies that are increasingly forced by global competition to adopt ultra-efficient ways of working. New re-engineering business processes require new skills. Therefore, the half-life of skills and jobs is shrinking fast.'

Champy goes on to suggest that there must be a new deal with employees (whatever their status) that spells out what they will have to do and what they will get for it. 'We need a new covenant with employees. If I can't guarantee you a job for life or even a job for good performance if your job is no longer needed, I must guarantee you something else to keep you when I do need your skills. That something else is your employability – either in my organization or some other.'

Continued development and growth

And Champy confirms what has already been suggested that, 'what I, as a manager, owe you as a worker, is your continued development and growth. I must give you the skills you need for the new jobs in my organization *or* the new jobs elsewhere. Otherwise, I won't be able to attract you to my organization in the first place and retain you if I want to.'

Ever the pragmatist, Champy points out that we are going to have to make some changes to compensation plans to make

> **Questions for beginners to the business game**
>
> Asked what he would do and what questions would he ask, if he was just starting out on his career, Peter Drucker – now in his sprightly eighties had this to say. 'First question, where can I get a job that is willing to pay for whatever skills I have? Second, am I learning something? Third, and a question – that to be frank – I didn't ask until I was in my forties, what are my strengths, where do I belong?'
>
> 'The one difference, and the one thing I hope young people will learn, is that they have to take responsibility for placing themselves. The first job you have is basically nothing but a place where you learn who you are and where you belong. It is a place where you find out what your strengths are and also what your personality is. From then on you have to take responsibility for placing yourself. There is no personality prop that can do that for you – that was the delusion of the 1950s. There is no counsellor who can do that for you – that was the delusion of the 1970s. You have to know who you are. You and those around you have to know who you are, what your strengths are, where you belong, and then you have to place yourself.'

this happen. 'Of course, this means that people will become more portable than they are today. To make that happen, we have to make employee benefits more portable – health insurance, retirement and so on. We don't want people hanging on because they won't get insured somewhere else.

'This is not just a liberal idea, it's a pragmatic idea. And it's not just a political issue, it's a management issue.' What Champy wants to get across is that this is a liberalization, a freeing-up of the individual. He or she is able to say, 'why should I stay with your company Mr Manager, if I have to invest in you *but* you can fire me tomorrow even though I'm performing extremely well? Why should I have any loyalty whatsoever?'

Of course, you can say that many consultants have worked like this for many years. But in fact in both the USA and Europe, their covenant has also been changed over the past years of recession. The security cushion, the guarantee of the monthly or annual retainer has disappeared never to return. So, indeed many others – not just middle managers – are in the 'anxious' not the 'overclass' or automatic survivors.

Here's another view – not all that far away from Champy's – of the covenant between employer and employee from outplacement specialist Win Nystrom who also feels that, 'the archaic illusion of security for loyalty was never really there to be broken. It is better said that a misperception has been resolved. But that previous "implied" relationship, or psychological bond represented more than the illusion of financial security. It provided a sense of belonging and a sense of worth and status.'

In redefining the job, the manager's role is going to be finding ways to keep the culture of the organization even though the rules have changed. Now that the employee has finally discovered that there never really were any rules, it is going to take a great deal of management talent to create real values in a company.

But it is possible to find ways to make the new-look organization work. Says Win Nystrom, in the new partnership agreement the employee, 'gives continued value-added services and genuine commitment to the mission and goals of the project he works on. In return the employer gives the employee pay for performance and employability.'

The reward package

And the 'pay' is more than monetary reward. Forecasts Nystrom, 'Payment will include, aside from cash, a cocktail of: further development of competencies, exposure to other "clients", access to technological systems, quality of work environment, consideration for dual careers and single parents and almost anything that is of value to the individual at the given moment.'

The key to the reward system is that employees continue to learn, increase their knowledge and boost their future employability.

 Work where you can increase your knowledge and raise your future employability status.

For the corporate high performer in the firm of 2010, Nystrom thinks the possibilities of reward are stratospheric. 'The compensation of high performers will be multiple choice. They will have the option to receive what is of value to them according to their personal circumstances. At one moment leverage performance base-pay would be appropriate, while others may prefer more predictable pay schedules. Choice of projects, telecommuting, flexible hours, access to technology, professional exposure and of course training. The essence is that the reward is specific to the performer and flexible over time.

But it isn't just the pay for performance factor that we will have to take into account. According to Françoise Bacq, a compensation specialist with consultants, Hewitt CBC in Brussels, the pay for performance bubble has already burst. This means that all of us must find new ways to reward the people we want to keep around.

Bacq comments, 'The reward system of the future is likely to be more trustworthy and respectful of the individual's potential and their natural willingness to develop their capabilities.' She adds, 'Total compensation packages will progressively be redesigned around the core concern of recognizing the individual's needs and potential and of treating them like adults, rather than like dependent kids.' (See Insight, page 140).

But there are a great many people who see that we are not out of the payment for performance trough yet. For many, it will, perhaps, be the only way to put enough cash and additional benefits together and build some much needed security.

Survival of the specialists

So the employee takes on an ever more mercenary role. Knowing that the circle of trust has not only be broken, but never actually existed will turn the advantage over to the specialists. As Nick Winkfield, of MORI points out, 'The key motivator for high performers will be high incomes and profit shares – not equity. Managers will expect to have forty years of retirement and no job security. Their pensions will consist of largely what they have managed to save and – unlike many current schemes – they will want to have full, personal control

> **Be independent!**
>
> If he was just beginning his working life again, the man who has led the re-engineering revolution, Jim Champy, says he would concentrate on being independent. Asked what type of career he would choose if he was twenty-years-old again, Champy responds, 'I would force myself to be independent, to learn how to make money on my own without working for a large company. Why? Because the new covenant says that there is no guarantee of employment.'
>
> Matching Peter Drucker's thoughts (see page 136) he continues, 'Also, by thinking of myself as being on my own, it forces me to gain skills in self-management, self-governance and self-direction – all of which are critical in working in re-engineered organizations. If you choose to work in one.'

over their savings. People are learning that, equity participation locks people into a company, but does not lock the company into them.'

A telling point is made by Philip Kotler, who questions whether as a contractor or specialist a person can ever feel dedicated to an organization when only motivated by pay. And he warns, 'specialists will be the most mobile of the labour pool, but we must remember that their allegiance may be stronger towards their profession.'

Jean-Claude Larreche believes that these different groups working for and with the corporation will call for three – very distinct – types of relationship. 'First, there will be the "star" contract, with the top performers who have a high market value and contribute to the organization much more than their direct cost; the organization has to deserve the loyalty of this individual in competition with other individuals. Second, the "development" contract for employees who are important contributors and in whom the organization has an interest to invest for mutual benefit. Third, the "support" contract for employees who have a role in supporting activities but are in a weak supply/demand situation and are therefore trying to gain loyalty from the employer.'

Where your pay-packet is going

Whatever else won't be the same in 2010, whoever employs us – full-time, part-time or on a contract – will still have to do one thing: pay us for our labours. So, just where are we going in trends in compensation over the next fifteen years. What can we all expect as our reward for a job well done? Françoise Bacq, a senior consultant with Hewitt CBC, one of Europe's leading executive compensation and benefit consultants has some very specific views of what's around the corner. 'Pay for performance programmes,' she suggests, 'are bound to fade away over the next ten to fifteen years, there has always been something fundamentally wrong about assuming that an individual would only give the best of himself if big money is put in front of his nose. In practical terms, this means that remuneration will no longer be structured by irrelevant factors such as seniority, promotion (what really matters is to grow not to go up) or past qualifications (what will count is the process of continuing one's development).'

Instead of these increasingly outmoded methods of reward, Bacq suggests that the package of tomorrow will be structured around three areas.

- The individual's material needs (allowing a fair budget for housekeeping, leisure, children's education), possibly based on national cost-of-living indicators.
- Personal training and development costs. Either amortizing past study costs, or the financing of new skill acquisition. this already implies that the new compensation structure will not recognize or reward existing competencies, but rather the on-going development of new skills. In other words it will encourage processes rather than status.
- The objective level of difficulty, risk and collective responsibility involved in the individual's assignment. What will matter here is the level of stress inherently imposed on the manager or specialist, not the actual level of initiative and personal involvement shown.'

Bacq further suggests that this package is going to be a very flexible form of reward system that meets the differing and

continued

changing needs of individuals. She says, 'Once the overall pay level is determined, the pay components within that package will then be allowed to meet – as closely as possible – the specifics of the employee's needs. That means that remuneration will be essentially flexible and that perquisites will cease to be status symbols. Depending on personal preferences and needs company cars and retirement premiums will be tradeable against vacation days or extended medical coverage at collectively negotiated rates. A core coverage of life risks will be insured collectively by the employer, but the individual will be encouraged to share that responsibility by a personal investment decision.'

But if performance-related pay is doomed to disappear from positive employer practices, profit sharing, according to Bacq, is set to come into its own as a reward medium. 'While pay for performance sends a negative message to managers, by its assumption that they wouldn't perform but for the money, profit sharing simply recognizes that employees are co-authors of the business success and naturally share with stockholders the right to eat some of the corporate cake.'

Finally, to get the reward equation correct, Bacq makes the point that all of us have to understand what performance really is, 'a continuous development of true self-confidence, of self-expression, of intellectual curiosity, of creativity as well as a sense of responsibility, initiative and risk taking.'

'These', suggests Bacq are 'behavioral traits that cannot be stimulated from without through purely material or financial rewards, but can only be encouraged through positive attitudes, genuine empowerment, open communication, the ability to fail and positive feedback.'

As we head for the new millennium, Bacq feels that, 'these are probably the ultimate reward that employees will be increasingly looking for.'

Get ready to boost your investment in training ... knowledge workers are going to be expensive.

The training burden

John Humble makes an important point when he raises the issue that for the employers – although they may be getting more for less in some areas right now as they tighten the productivity screws – the increased investment in training and development will be an ever bigger bubble on the budget, that they had better make early provisions for. 'Companies who want to attract the best people will have to deliver continuous learning opportunities for this self development. The investment in training in new skills and knowledge, as well as learning from one another, will be a major increase in cost. But if you think this is a bad investment, work out the true costs of ignorance in this new knowledge world of the next millennium.'

Humble – despite all that is happening in our organizations – remains optimistic about the future. 'Every person and every organization has the chance to invent their own future. The entrepreneurial, well managed, totally competitive organizations always win through, even in discouraging situations. It is the very poor and marginal, with neither the will or competence to become world-class competitors, who will disappear.'

Manage change – don't let it manage you

Lastly, a word of warning about change. Everything that you have read in this book points to the need for all of us – as individuals and as organizations – to embrace change, to make it a constant companion, an on-going part of our lives. While there is no doubt that it should be, we must be pragmatic and explain that change isn't something that happens every day from Monday to Friday.

Looking at most corporations – even those with an enviable track record of innovation – change, and the need for change, has always been tempered with the need for stability as well. A closer look at those successful businesses also reveals that most change (particularly the major pieces of reorganization and rejuvenation) are done in short, highly focused spurts, followed by a period of stability.

It is important for all of us to keep in mind that there is a danger of confusing innovation with change. They are not –

and will never be – the same thing. Innovation is a constant process that provides us with new products, processes and services: it is vital to our future. Change is something that shakes the organizational tree, perhaps even sends a shockwave or two through the foundations. That is something that is necessary from time to time, but none of us need constant seismic shocks. Stability, knowing where the organization is going and why is equally important: indeed that sort of atmosphere actively encourages innovation.

So, take care with change. There are many times when it is necessary, but don't change for change's sake. Recognize the need, carry it out, then remember that stability to grow and innovate has an equal place in the corporation of tomorrow.

What to watch for

- Face squarely the issue of change, but be rational about it. Remember it has to be right for your organization and you have to balance change and stability not just tear down the structure for the sake of it.
- The mythical contract between employer and employee of a job for life is smashed. Don't let anyone tell you different. Every manager, every specialist is on his or her own.
- The new working agreement between employer and employee will offer variety, opportunity and reward for those prepared to embrace it. Now's the time to make a start.
- Companies will have one responsibility: guaranteeing employability when they no longer need them.
- Work where you get the best training and development to ensure your future survival.
- Compensation won't be just about cash, but a menu of options that meet individual needs. But, careers will be shorter, so look to earn more, faster than ever before.
- If you're running a company expect training and development costs to balloon. Failure to develop people will ensure a poor quality workforce and a poor reputation that will stifle future recruitment.

Conclusion

Going to work in 2010 will be rather like working in Hollywood for the movie industry. There are the stars, and their agents, the producers, the directors, the stand-ins, understudies, stunt men and extras. There are the technicians, the electricians, the cameramen, the cutters, the wardrobe, the casting and location specialists: a myriad of talent and temperaments. The producer is the manager who brings them all together, who pays the money and makes the team work. The director is the genius who takes the idea and converts it into reality. Each of the actors and the support staff has a profession, each a specialization, each a talent. All are rewarded according to their ability. When the movie's finished, the team is wound up. Some of them may work together again, some may not. That's what the modern corporation is going to demand of all of us, whether we sit in the producer's office, the director's chair, the star's trailer or just somewhere on the set. And if we are part of a team that produces a product the customer likes, we might be asked back to try and do it again.

If the analogy of the movie industry doesn't do much for your imagination, think of the other flat organizations you know of, orchestras, operas, soccer teams. In terms of being truly delayered, dealing with available technology, working at the cutting edge of new developments, on a constant learning curve and highly innovative, possibly nothing comes closer to the microcosm of tomorrow's corporation than a Formula One or Indy Car racing team. There is a boss, a few top managers and a whole panoply of specialists. That's what the delayered organization looks like. That's what is waiting for all of us.

Can it be managed on a larger scale? Yes, it would seem so. As the central core – the permanent cadre of management – shrink, as unproductive parts are sold off and many non-vital departments and services are outsourced, there won't be so many people around anyway. Information technology can take care of much of the rest.

While many of the management specialists talk of radical change and paradigm shifts, much of what they are suggesting is really making modern, international corporations look much the same as many successful examples of alternative structures we see all around us if we bother to look. Many of these examples have been around for centuries. It isn't that we ignored them either. It is just that – until now – we didn't need them for our ever-expanding, ever-complex organizational structures. Now that all that has changed – for most of us – these unchanged organizational structures might have some use to us again. More probably, they will be adapted by each of us to suit our own, specialized needs.

The question we must all ask ourselves: whether an owner, a senior manager, a specialist or a business student is, 'As we head into the next millennium, do I want to be a part of a successful organization, or one that is suffering from terminal blindness?'

This book gives some ideas of where business is going and outlines the challenges for managers in the next millennium. Let's hope we have the vision and courage and the enthusiasm to face them.

Biographies

Many of the contributors and those quoted in the book, kindly gave their time for lengthy in-depth interviews. To help the reader in identifying them and their expertise in the business world, the following short biographies have been included.

Thomas Bonoma was Executive Vice-President of Benckiser GmbH, a privately held German producer of cleaning products and cosmetics until mid-1993. He left Benckiser to apply his principles for marketing implementation to his personal acquisition and consulting activities.

At Harvard, Bonoma held the rank of full Professor of Business Administration and he taught marketing in the School's Advanced Management Programme, designed for senior executives.

His recent books include *Marketing Management*, *Marketing Performance*, *The Marketing Edge: Making Strategies Work*, *Managing Marketing: Text and Cases*, *Psychology for Management*, and *The Executive Survival Manual*.

James A. Champy is a leading author, expert and strategist on the role of information and information technology in business. Co-founder of CSC Index, Champy provides counsel to many major multinational corporations seeking to capitalize on the competitive potential of these technologies. His recent bestseller, *Re-engineering the Corporation: A Manifesto for Business Revolution*, delves deep into the most important topic in business circles today: re-engineering.

George Day is the Geoffrey T. Boisi Professor of Marketing and Director of the Huntsman Centre for Global Competition and Leadership at the Wharton School of the University of Pennsylvania. He previously taught at the University of Western Ontario, Stanford University, IMEDE (International Management

Development Institute) in Lausanne, Switzerland, and the University of Toronto and has held visiting appointments at the Harvard Graduate School of Business Administration and the Sloan School of Management at MIT.

Professor Day is editor of the West Publishing series on Strategic Market Management, was previously the section editor for Strategy and Planning for the *Journal of Marketing*. He has authored ten books in the areas of marketing and strategic business planning. His most recent book is *Market Driven Strategy: Processes for Creating Value*.

Peter Drucker is a truly international figure in the field of management organization and economic and business policy. He has written 27 books and numerous articles which have been translated into 20 languages and is the recipient of 22 honorary doctorates by universities all over the world. His classic books include, *The Effective Executive, The Frontiers of Management*, and *The Practice of Management*. In his most recent book, *Post-Capitalist Society*, he details the immense social transition our society is going through, and helps the reader understand this transformation's impact on business, labour and management. Since 1971 Drucker has served as Clarke Professor of Social Science and Management at Claremont Graduate School in California, which, in 1987, named its Graduate Management Centre after him.

Liam Fahey is Adjunct Professor of Strategic Management at Babson College (USA) and Visiting Professor of Strategic Management at the Cranfield School of Management (UK). Previously, he taught at Northwestern University's J.L. Kellogg Graduate School of Management and at Boston University.

Professor Fahey's area of specialization is Strategic Management. His research and teaching centre on competitive and political strategy, and macro-environmental and competitor analysis.

He has (co)authored three books: *Energy Management in Industrial Firms* (1984), *The New Competition: What Theory Z Didn't Tell You About-Marketing* (1985), and *Macro-environmental Analysis for Strategic Management* (1986).

Sumantra Ghoshal is Professor of Strategy and Management at INSEAD. He is the Faculty Director for Managing the

Multinational Enterprise and Executive Forum, two of INSEAD's top management programmes. He has published five books including *Managing Across Borders* and *Transnational Management*, both co-authored with Professor Christopher A. Bartlett. He has won the 'Outstanding Teacher Of the Year' Award at INSEAD and his cases have twice won the 'European Case of the Year' Award from the European Case Clearing House. Professor Ghoshal serves on the Editorial Boards of the *Strategic Management Journal* and the *Journal of International Business Studies* and is a member of the Advisory Board of the Carnegie-Bosch Institute.

Donald Hambrick is Samuel Bronfman Professor of Democratic Business Enterprise and Director of the Executive Leadership Research Center at the Graduate School of Business, Columbia University. He is the author of numerous articles, chapters, and books on the topics of strategy formulation, organizational design, executive staffing and incentives, and the composition and development of top management teams.

John Humble is an international management consultant. He is also a Director of Minit Corporation and Dun Consulting Services and Corporate Adviser to Digital Equipment Company, United Kingdom. John Humble's books include *Improving Business Results, Managing by Objectives in Action, The Effective Computer* (with C. Grindley), *The Experienced Manager, How to Manage by Objectives,* and *The Social Responsibility of Business and The Responsible Multinational Enterprise. Business Magazine* cited John Humble as one of the 24 'Makers of Modern Management'.

Paul G. Kahn, while serving as President and Chief Executive Officer of AT&T's Universal Card Services (UCS), masterminded one of the most successful financial services start-ups of the decade. Under Mr Kahn's leadership, Universal Card grew into the world's largest issuer of MasterCard credit cards in less than four years. The company achieved profitability ahead of schedule, became a Fortune 100 sized company with over a billion dollars of annual revenue, and won the 1992 'Malcolm Baldrige National Quality Award' – the youngest company and only financial services company ever to do so.

Dr Mike Kami was the chief strategic planner for IBM and Xerox during their super-growth years. He retired young and moved to Florida many years ago. But he couldn't just stand still. He became a one-man mini-conglomerate: a combination consultant, writer, public speaker, motorcycle rider, publisher, yachtsman and entrepreneur. He is considered one of the leading business advisers in the world and also one of the most expensive. He was featured in many magazines and publications in USA and abroad. He is knowledgeable, down-to-earth and tells it as it is. Peter Drucker and Tom Peters called him the best planner they know.

T.W. Kang is Managing Director of Global Synergy Associates. He has authored two books on the Pacific Rim, *Gaishi, The Foreign Company in Japan* and *Is Korea the next Japan?* He has lectured widely on issues relating to the Pacific Rim through the American Electronics Association, the Ministry of International Trade and Industry of Japan, JETRO, Keidanren, the Executive Training Program of the European Community. He has appeared as guest commentator on Cable News Network and NHK. Previous to his current position, Mr Kang spent a decade at Intel Corporation in a variety of capacities. His most recent position with Intel was System Group General Manager for Intel Japan in which he was responsible for the product adaptation, marketing, quality assurance, maintenance, training and sales of Intel's system products including OEM personal computers, parallel supercomputers and real-time, industrial computers.

Philip Kotler is the S.C. Johnson & Son Distinguished Professor of International Marketing at the J.L. Kellogg Graduate School of Management, Northwestern University. Philip Kotler is author of the most widely used marketing book in leading business schools worldwide, *Marketing Management: Analysis, Planning, Implementation and Control*. Professor Kotler was the first recipient of the American Marketing Association's (AMA) 'Distinguished Marketing Educator Award'. In addition, the AMA conferred on him the further honour of 'Leader in Marketing Thought'. The European Association of Marketing Consultants and Sales Trainers awarded Kotler their 'Prize for Marketing Excellence'.

Jean-Claude Larréché is Professor of Marketing at INSEAD and a specialist on strategic marketing. In 1989, he was the recipient of the 'INSEAD Professor of the Year' award which was created by the INSEAD Alumni Association. He is President of Strat*X,, a company specializing in strategic management development and educational technology, member of the Board of Reckitt & Colman plc, London and of Gemini Consulting.

Henri Mintzberg has developed his reputation not by popularizing new techniques, but by rethinking the fundamentals of strategy and structure, management and planning. He published a prize-winning book on structure that significantly altered how we think about designing organizations. This book was used by General Electric, Procter and Gamble, Pepsico, and just recently Ford when they were reorganizing.

His latest book *The Rise and Fall of Strategic Planning*, questions the process that has mesmerized so many organizations. Dr Mintzberg was President of the Strategic Management Society from 1988 to 1991, the premier grouping of practitioners and researchers in the field worldwide.

He has consulted to an unusual range of organizations, from the Dutch Police Force to Greenpeace, and in recent months, from the very largest, such as Shell and Ford, to the rather small, including Frontec, the Canadian firm that staffs the Arctic warning stations.

Michael E. Porter is the C. Roland Christensen Professor of Business Administration at the Harvard Business School and a leading authority on competitive strategy. Professor Porter joined the Harvard Business School faculty in 1973, and became one of the youngest tenured professors in the School's history. His ideas have now become basis for one of the required courses at the School. Professor Porter is the author of 13 books and over 45 articles. His book, *Competitive Strategy: Techniques for Analysing Industries and Competitors*, published in 1980, is widely recognized as the leading work in its field. In its 45th printing, it has been translated into 15 languages.

Professor Porter has served as a counsellor on competitive strategy to many leading US and international companies, among them AT&T, Campbell's Soup, Credit Suisse, First Boston, DuPont, Montedison, Procter & Gamble, Royal Dutch Shell and Westinghouse.

Louis W. Stern is the co-author of *Marketing Channels, Management in Marketing Channels, Legal Aspects of Marketing Strategy: Antitrust and Consumer Protection Issues, Managerial Analysis in Marketing* and *Competition in the Marketplace*. He is an adviser to such companies as IBM, General Electric, Eastman Kodak, Motorola, Ford, Xerox, Ameritech, Kodak, Boise Cascada, Mead, the International Strategic Forum of the Direct Marketing Association and the American Medical Association.

Lou Stern is the John D. Gray Distinguished Professor of Marketing at the J.L. Kellogg Graduate School of Management, Northwestern University. He has served as the Ford Foundation Visiting Professor at Harvard Business School, a faculty associate of the Hernstein Institute, Vienna, and a visiting professor at the Norwegian School of Economics and Business Administration in Bergen.

Lester Thurow is a world-renowned author and a distinguished professor of management and economics who has taught at MIT for more than 20 years. Previously the Dean of MIT's Sloan School of Management, Thurow is currently on a two-year leave. The vice president of the American Economics Association, he is author of several widely acclaimed books including the bestsellers *The Zero-Sum Society* and *The Zero-Sum Solution*, that advocate the need for a more competitive US economy. Thurow's newest book, *Head-to-Head: The Coming Economic Battle Among Japan, Europe and America*, was on *The New York Times* bestseller list for more than six months.

Paul Tiffany is a Professor of Management and fellow of the Aresty Institute of Executive Education at The Wharton School of the University of Pennsylvania. Prior to joining the Wharton faculty, Professor Tiffany served as a Lecturer at the Graduate School of Business, Stanford University, where he taught courses in marketing management.

N. (Venkat) Venkatraman is Associate Professor of Management at the School of Management at Boston University. From July 1985 until December 1993, he was on the faculty at the Sloan School of Management at Massachusetts Institute of Technology. At Boston University

Systems Research Center, he is leading a multicompany research programme at the interface between strategic management and information technology. His research and teaching interests lie at the interface between strategic management and information technology, with a particular focus on business transformation enabled through IT capabilities.